Grade
4

Connie, age nine.

Grade
5

Betsy, age ten.

Grade
6

Kathy, age eleven.

EMPHASIS: ART

A QUALITATIVE PROGRAM FOR THE ELEMENTARY SCHOOL

A collage mural (4' x 16') made from construction paper as a group project (grade 2).

FRANK WACHOWIAK
Professor of Art
University of Iowa

in collaboration with

THEODORE RAMSAY
Assistant Professor of Art
University of Iowa

EMPHASIS: ART

A QUALITATIVE PROGRAM FOR THE ELEMENTARY SCHOOL

INTERNATIONAL TEXTBOOK COMPANY
Scranton, Pennsylvania

INTERNATIONAL TEXTBOOKS IN ART AND ART EDUCATION

Italo L. de Francesco
Consulting Editor

Third Printing
August, 1966

To children everywhere who make the teaching of art a constant adventure.

EDITOR'S FOREWORD

Professors Wachowiak and Ramsay have collaborated on a long awaited project—a qualitative art program for the elementary schools.

The term qualitative applies not only to the well-conceived selection of activities suggested but also to the illustrations which are included in the text. In a real sense, the "qualitative" program presented by the authors is readily recognized as being founded on a sane philosophy of art education—devoid of clichés, obscure meanings, and debatable issues.

Experience and experimentation in the classrooms in all activities introduced ensures the elementary teacher that these things actually did happen, that they are real. This virtue of the text is a further warranty of what the authors have achieved with children under their sympathetic guidance. In the same spirit, they can be achieved in the typical classroom.

Finally, the brevity of the authors' exposition of their philosophy of art education is commendable in a book which is primarily intended to *help* teachers who actually labor with children from day to day.

I. L. DE FRANCESCO

AUTHORS' PREFACE

This book concerns itself first and foremost with the adventure and science of *teaching art* to children. It is not a "let the child do as he pleases" book, nor is it a text on "how to do it in two easy lessons." It is dedicated simply to the task of discovering and developing the *art in children's art*.

The authors suggest it as a guide for the classroom teacher who wishes tangible help in enriching the art program. They also recommend it as a text for the college student who is looking for a candid and unequivocal blueprint of qualitative elementary school art practices. They offer it as a straightforward description of a plan-of-action for the veteran artist-teacher who seeks continuing challenges, new techniques, and classroom-tested approaches for his repertoire.

Readers of this book will find themselves constantly reminded of one of the authors' strongest beliefs: that a creative, intelligent teacher with firm, aesthetic convictions is the most important factor in a qualitative art program. They believe that this person should have an adequate studio and art history background and that he must continually involve himself in some personal creative activity in order to continue as a successful teacher of art.

A major and significant part of the success of a qualitative elementary art program is the unselfish and deliberate involvement of the teacher. Constant thinking, planning, dreaming, organizing, experimenting, motivating, and evaluating are the challenging requisites of dedicated teaching, but the growing confidence and contagious exuberance of the children in expressing their reactions and ideas in an aesthetic framework is worth all the extra concern and time the teacher must bring to his assignment.

Another basic conviction the authors hold is that children from the first grade on up can benefit from a program where art fundamentals are taught and not left to chance. The harangue over process versus product has degenerated into ambiguous double-talk. Wherever the process of discovery and creation is founded on strong aesthetic principles, the product will be worthwhile as well. It is impossible to separate the two. Corroborative evidence abounds that we have too long underestimated the art capacities of young children and have barely begun to tap their intuitive, expressive potential.

The time has come for an honest and realistic reappraisal of the purposes and objectives of the art program in the elementary school. Art educators, artists, and aestheticians have been most explicit, both in speech and in print, in directing our attention to the creeping emasculation of the visual arts in our schools, but few of them have proposed anything but theoretical and generalized alternatives. What the teachers of elementary art classes need are some clear directives, some sharp specifics and constants, and some fundamental concepts to give purpose, continuity, validity, and structure to their teaching. It is hoped that this text will provide the definitive guidance they seek.

The spirit, theory, and procedure of teaching art to children which form the basis of this book have been the hallmark of the art education program at the State University of Iowa and its University Schools for the past fifteen years. The emphasis, philosophically speaking, has always been on ART—art as an adventure, as a discipline, and as a science with its own special vocabulary, its own singular skills, its own unique core of learnings, and its own incomparable rewards.

All illustrations, unless otherwise identified, are works by children from the University Elementary School, State University of Iowa, Iowa City. All color photography was done by the authors; black and white photography by James Kent, State University of Iowa.

FRANK WACHOWIAK
THEODORE K. RAMSAY

Iowa City, Iowa
June, 1964

Table of Contents

Chapter 1

Linoleum print (grade 3).

The teaching of art in the elementary schools today is as richly rewarding a profession as any human being could have when it is done with understanding, purpose, planning, conviction, and love. It is the teacher's responsibility to build the child's confidence by guiding him from one plateau to another until he develops aesthetic concepts. If nothing is said to the child about the principles and elements of design, it is presumptuous to assume that he will develop in art awareness.

Chapter 3

Linoleum print (grade 5).

A creative, imaginative, sympathetic, and constantly resourceful teacher is *sine qua non* in the development and maintenance of a qualitative program in elementary art. He is the prime catalyst and the bridge builder, and it is his responsibility to develop a climate of affection and permissiveness, of order and rationale, and of excitement and creativity.

Chapter 2

Linoleum print (grade 5).

Children are inquisitive and observant. They are susceptible to influences every waking moment of their lives, but they are not always discriminating, and quite often the trite and tasteless object gets as much of their approval as the well-designed product. What a qualitative art program can do, in some measure, is to help them be more selective, more discerning, and more expressive in the many important choices they will make in their lives.

Chapter 4

Linoleum print (grade 3).

Inspiration for the youngster's art expression may come from his experiences at home, in the community, and on the playground; from trips and visits to museums, zoos, garden, and national parks; or from movies, television, radio, books, and periodicals. The responsibility for reactivating these experiences and giving them an immediacy that will trigger the youngster into an art expression is the teacher's, and his alone.

Chapter 5

leum print (grade 5).

PLANNING A PROGRAM.....35

A well-planned sequence of creative projects, based upon the teacher's developed aesthetic convictions and on his understanding of the child's interests, needs, and expressive potential, is both core and foundation of the qualitative program in art, a program which provides a variety of challenges in a wide range of exciting materials, allows for art sessions long enough for real involvement in a problem or technique, and provides the child with multiple opportunities to explore, experiment, select, organize, and appreciate.

Chapter 7

Linoleum print (grade 3).

FUNDAMENTAL ART CONCEPTS REVIEWED 133

constant and recurring compositional principles in all aspects of the fine arts, past and present, should form the core of college art education offerings. A similar fundamentals approach in classroom teaching can prove to be the most stabilizing and most significant approach in a qualitative art program. The best art is almost always the result of many hours, many years of mastering a style and technique, of ordering the vision, and of integrating mind, heart, and hand.

Chapter 6

leum print (grade 5).

A PROGRAM IN ACTION.....53

Fundamental art experiences in a variety of media, including motivational aspects, techniques, and suggestions for aesthetic evaluation. Drawing the figure, landscape, animals, and still life. Painting with tempera. Tempera batik. Mural making. Collage. Tissue collage. Mosaics. Printmaking with vegetables, cardboard, and linoleum. Crayon. Crayon engraving and resist. Clay and clay-plaster reliefs. Sculpture in plaster. Box sculpture. Masks.

Appendices A to G

Linoleum print by a college education major.

APPENDICES.........147

A. The Child: His Characteristics
B. The Child: His Natural Development in Art
C. Recommended Reference Books, Bulletins, and Periodicals
D. Recommended Films, Color Slides, Reproductions, and Recordings
E. Materials
F. Facilities for Elementary Art
G. Glossary of Terms

Kathy, age six.

John, age six.

The developmental drawings illustrated above and elsewhere in the text can provide the teacher with graphic evidence of the child's growth in visual expression. At the beginning of each school year the children in each grade are asked to make a drawing of themselves in the act of combing their hair, brushing their teeth, playing ball, or a similar activity. These are usually done in pencil or black crayon. A brief discussion before the drawing begins is devoted to what action they might perform, what they might be wearing, and where they might be. However, once the youngsters begin to draw, no further suggestions are made, either in regard to the experience they are portraying or to the composition of the drawing itself. They are allowed to work on the drawing for as long as it takes them to complete it.

BASIC PREMISES

The teaching of art in the elementary schools today is as richly rewarding a profession as any human being could have when it is done with understanding, purpose, planning, conviction, and love. It is a privilege, a revelation, and a joy to observe children create in paint, crayon, chalk, clay, and paper. Their imaginative scope and compositional daring know no bounds. Is it any wonder then that their intuitive and naïve expressions have entranced and even influenced painters like Henri Matisse, Paul Klee, Pablo Picasso, Jean Dubuffet, Joan Miró, and Enrico Baj?

To watch a child, sensitively nurtured and guided, develop in drawing and coloring ability from simple to complex interpretations is to witness a most fascinating aspect of human growth. Yet without a wise teacher's help and encouragement, a youngster may stay on the same creative plateau for years. His command of line, of form, of color, of pattern, and of composition may remain static or quite possibly retrogress, leading to his eventual discouragement, frustration, and apathy.

Stimulated by a teacher's challenging motivations, the child learns to see more, to sense more, to be more vitally aware of his environment, and consequently to organize his ideas in a more expressive, personal form. The teacher of art should begin very early

talking to the growing child about the possibilities of design and composition. Children are more inquisitive, more alert, and more discerning than we have been led to believe. The teacher may have to substitute simpler learning terms for the younger children, but he will find that they understand quite readily the ideas of using light and dark colors, of creating big and small shapes, of repeating something over and over again to make patterns, and of making things go together to fill the space. It is the teacher's responsibility to build the child's confidence by guiding him from one plateau to another to develop aesthetic concepts, repeating when necessary those art principles that strengthen his confidence and give purpose to his performance.

We have been bombarded too many times by the misleading assumption that anything a child draws is "art." It may be, admittedly, a child's drawing, but it is not always art. Children with imagination, sensitivity, heightened perception, and vivid recall, who express their experiences and their reactions with a feeling ordered and disciplined by compositional structure and design, create *art.* For the majority of children this sense of design, of composition, of order, and of an aesthetic form must be learned or "caught" from their teachers, their parents, and their neighbors; from visits to art museums; from fine books, magazines, films, and television programs; from continuous contact with fine art, real or reproduced; and from well-designed products at home, at school, and in the community.

Mural done with felt nib marker and watercolors (grades 2 and 3).

2

Too often what we call art in children's drawings is not the aesthetic form of art as we know it, but a simple graphic expression by the child that can be more readily compared to basic writing than to creative literature. Fine art expression is more akin to poetry, and there are many recorded instances of children in the elementary schools creating delightful, sparkling poetic verse. A basic written statement such as "I live in a house" can be compared, for example, to a simple drawing of a nondescript house in the middle of the page. Let us ask a child to tell us where he lives in a poetic way, and he might say:

My house is sunny white with a green roof.
It peeks through two big willows,
And a blue door in front says "Come in."

A bushy hedge goes round my house,
And red tulips hug the porch
Where I sit in a swing and say "Come in."

The poetic spirit gives life to the pictorial version when the teacher encourages and nurtures the perceptive, inquisitive, and sensitive nature of the child. The house then becomes not just a stereotype in the middle of the paper, but a personal place, individual and unique. It may be a house made of fancy brick, rough stone, clapboard, redwood, or cast cement, with chimneys, shutters iron railings, breezeways, carports, windvanes, television antennae, lantern posts, picture windows, creeping vines, pierced screens, winding sidewalks, picket fences, window boxes, or sculptured hedges.

In poetry we find that the quality of our interpretation or expression depends on the most expressive word or phrase, on effective alliteration, on meter or rhythm, and sometimes on rhyme. In the art expressions of children, too, we discover a blending of art principles and fundamentals leading to unity of organization and to a strong design structure which distinguishes them from ordinary and impoverished representations.

In almost every contemporary text on teaching art to children we find an emphasis on the teacher's duty to help the youngsters achieve worthwhile and rich experiences in order to have something to say, to draw, to paint, to print, to sculpt, or to construct. Sometimes the teacher helps the children recall an event or impression of their past. More often he provides a new experience through a field trip, a model brought to class, a dramatization, a film, or a poem. But for qualitative or consummate teaching in art, this is not enough. The teacher must also learn to guide the children and to interpret their experiences in an ordered, more aesthetic framework. The child's expression of an impact or an occasion must be fused with the fundamentals of structure, design, and composition in order to be *art*.

Every time a child is guided to create or compose a painting, a mural, or a print, he is usually encouraged to make many aesthetic evaluations of his work which subtly aid him in his progressive steps toward criteria of taste and discernment. If nothing is said to the youngster about design, structure, form, emphasis, line, rhythm, repetition, variety within unity, the myriad moods and facets of color, texture, pattern, contrast, and space, it is presumptuous for us to assume that he will develop in art awareness. In the chapter "Avenues to Motivation" various methods for guiding children to achieve their highest art potential are described and analyzed.

We are surfeited with the admonitions of art educators, psychologists, and guidance experts who tell us in periodicals, lectures, and textbooks that it is easy to teach art to children. They speak of "relatively little effort required," or "this is not hard to do—I can do this," or "to be creative, children need only materials and a place to work!" Why delude ourselves? *Art is not an easy subject to teach.* Nor is it an enigma without solution. Naturally it requires as much preparation, planning, guidance, and technical know-how as any other subject in school—as much indeed and more! And because such a high premium is put on preserving the individuality of the child's expression, the teacher must learn, too, to teach the language, the vocabulary, and the fundamentals of art, in such a permissive way that each child can benefit from the orientation without endangering his unique interpretation or delineation.

The child who draws, paints, or constructs will create more exciting, more fully-realized artwork when he perceives more and when he is made more aware of and more sensitive to his environment. If his contact with nature is superficial, if he only half sees the possibilities, if his identification with an experience is weak, or if he is intellectually lazy, then he is apt to be content with a shorthand version of an experience or an event. A stereotyped interpretation, such as the two curved lines for a bird in flight, a stick and sausage figure, or a lollypop tree, is seldom a perceived or meaningful one.

The teacher must be prepared to help the child react more sensitively, respond more fully, and distinguish unique characteristics more readily and effectively. This kind of guidance and stimulation is only one part of a complex job of motivation, but without it the child's expressions tend to be pauperized and sterile. Suggestions for rich motivation of experience and recall applicable to a variety of projects will be found in Chapter 4.

Teachers are continually cautioned not to impose adult standards on children's art efforts. This is understandable and commendable. *There are some standards, however, based on aesthetic considerations that the teacher should use as criteria.* These involve design, composition, and basic art structure, ranging from simple and elementary guideposts in the primary grades to complex and subtle injunctions in the upper grades. This kind of instruction does not burden the child with an adult concept but enriches his expression with an artistic awareness and a vision which develops intuition, insight, imagination, and an understanding based on the essence of things.

Very often what some art education analysts describe in awe as a child's unique way of seeing is already an artificially and pragmatically-influenced pattern of expression or interpretation, affected, biased, and regimented by adult (parent) tastes and by coy, stereotyped illustrations in coloring books, story and comic books, and school workbooks. It remains the job of the teacher of the art class to minimize these early impressions by presenting the child with a whole new series of art-oriented experiences based on fundamentally aesthetic considerations and premises, so that the child will get a chance to express his ideas in a significant form.

Another basic consideration is that the art program or curriculum should not be diluted and emasculated until it has no core, no substance, and no integrity of its own. When the art period is given too little time in the total school program, when it plays second fiddle to every other subject in the classroom, and when it is bogged down in a continuous demand for posters, signs, charts, stage decorations, table favors, and factually dominated dioramas, it is no longer a valid and meaningful art program. It is senseless to justify its inclusion in the elementary school curriculum on this basis. Either it has a body of vital subject matter and skills to be mastered, or it hasn't; either it has merit as a unique avenue to mental, social, and personal growth through creative action, or it hasn't. We believe it has.

Still another distinct handicap to a qualitative art program is the continued emphasis on misguided correlation practices where teachers use art to make other school subjects more palatable and in the process often kill the child's love for art. But even

here, there is much confusion among the writings of some of our art educators. We find them warning us against letting art become the slave of other areas in one breath and in the next suggesting a project of realistic clay vegetables to be used in a consumer's math project.

Often the articles in art education periodicals would lead one to believe that art teachers are afraid to voice their aesthetic convictions or to admit that they are influencing the youngsters for fear of being labeled old-fashioned or dictatorial. Any experienced, intelligent, and perceptive teacher of elementary art can ascertain after seeing a school exhibit of children's paintings or drawings whether an instructor's creative, guiding hand is evident in the results, no matter how many times the catalog may state "the children decided." All that an ingenious cover-up like this proves is that too many art teachers are confused about their roles in the education of children and afraid to say "I teach!"

It appears we are playing all positions of the game in trying to ingratiate ourselves with the psychologists, sociologists, psychiatrists, anthropologists, guidance counselors, administrators, and curriculum coordinators. We can learn much from every one of these specialists, but we must not forget that we are teachers of art. Let us do that one job well, so that the children placed in our charge grow in aesthetic awareness, in sensitivity to their changing world, in good taste, in creative potential, and in the intelligent appreciation of the art of the past, as well as the art

of their day. Art in the elementary school is justified only as long as it contributes effectively and purposefully to the *aesthetic, perceptive, and creative growth* of every child enrolled.

Until a teacher has taught a class of thirty or forty children all day long for a number of years, often under the most adverse conditions, it is impossible for him to predict what can or cannot be done in a typical teaching situation. We hear too frequently from art educators, long absent from today's elementary school situation, advising us "to let the child create," "it's the process not the product that counts," or "teach the child, not the technique." A teacher faced with today's overloaded classes does well indeed if he manages simply to keep the class under control so that learning takes place. He can maintain a working equilibrium as long as the children sense the purpose of the project or the direction of the effort. When youngsters feel they are not growing in mastery of a vocabulary, of facts as tools, of processes, and of techniques, they lose interest, and the stage is set for general disorder. Show us a class where the teacher "lets the child do as he pleases," and we will show you a class where a minimum of developmental learning is taking place.

The art program in the elementary school will continue to receive and deserve its share of the critic's scorn as long as the majority of young classroom teachers who leave our institutions of higher learning are so meagerly versed in the theory and fundamentals of art.

Pen and ink sketch made from a class model (grade 6).

Adequate and high-caliber college orientation in art history and art teaching methodology and experience in art techniques should provide the classroom teacher or the teacher of art with the background he requires:

> To plan the art program in terms of the youngsters' interests and needs,
> To understand the developmental stages of children's art growth,
> To provide and organize the necessary art materials and tools,
> To make available a variety of motivational resources,
> To allot the working space and time necessary to complete the projects,
> To renew the children's interest at critical stages,
> To recognize the technical aspects of more complex art media,
> To evaluate each child's work in terms of the youngster's own potential,
> To display the children's finished products to the best advantage, and at every opportunity
> To guide the youngsters towards the highest aesthetic standards.

The best teacher of art, however, will not rest on his college laurels alone. He will continue to augment and enrich his background year after year through further study, further experimentation, and further creativity. He will continue to learn from the children in his classes, from his peers, from his travels, and from readings and research, and with this new understanding, he will begin to realize how much is still undiscovered and how wide the horizons are.

Janice, age eight.

Jimmy, age seven.

THE CHILD AND HIS ENVIRONMENT

Children the world over have much in common. Before they are influenced and molded by their particular environments, they react alike to various stimuli, natural and artificial. They laugh; they cry; they delight in seeing and moving colorful objects; and they respond to sympathetic voices.

Very young children in all countries draw in much the same manner at similar age levels. They begin with scribbles, move to simple symbols, and progress to characteristic and naturalistic interpretation. They do all this instinctively. This does not imply that they are making artistic creations because what they express so spontaneously is usually done subconsciously with a naïveté that defies analysis. It is a form of basic communication comparable to a matter-of-fact conversation the child might carry on with others or with himself.

No two children are exactly alike. Even twins, who may confuse their teacher with their outward similarity, have different personalities, different reactions to their environment, and different mental abilities. The unique characteristics of children should

be a major guiding element for the teacher of art. This means that he must not expect the same response, the same skill, or the same interpretation from any two children, although they may be of the same age. Since the children have diverse interests, they should have an opportunity to participate in a variety of art projects. The youngster who excels in clay manipulation may respond less enthusiastically to drawing. The child who confidently tackles brush and paint may need more guidance in three-dimensional constructions.

A considered analysis of the developmental drawings found on the inside covers and facing the opening page of each chapter in this book will reveal that every child has his own visual interpretation for the human figure. Children are inquisitive and observant, it is true. They miss little in their daily experiences. They are susceptible to influences every waking moment of their lives, but they are not always discriminating, and quite often the very trite and tasteless object gets as much of their attention and approval as the well-designed, well-composed product. It is a major responsibility of the art teacher and the school to guide the child toward more aesthetic choices and to provide him with a wealth of appreciatory experiences in the fine arts.

Children in school need the understanding, approbation, guidance, and direction of a sympathetic teacher. They also thrive on the friendship, the approval, the spirited competition, and the intellectual rivalry of their classmates. To grow, the child must

10

TOP—Opaque watercolor, Burmese child art (grade 2).
CENTER—Crayon drawing by a Burmese child (grade 4).
BOTTOM—Tempera painting by a Burmese child (grade 6).

have emotional security, self-confidence, developmental challenges, an inquisitive nature, and a nurturing environment at home and in school.

Since no two children are exactly alike, it is difficult to say what a first grader is like or what a fifth grader is like. They often come from different backgrounds; they usually have had different experiences. Yet in order to understand them and to help them grow in art, the teacher must rely on some pertinent characteristics that have been identified as peculiar to certain age groups by psychologists, anthropologists, doctors, sociologists, general educators, parents, and teachers. If the teacher knows these characteristics, he will be in a better position to understand the children's behavior and potential. For a detailed description of these characteristics, see Appendices A and B. A word of caution is in order, however, for the characteristics which are listed there are merely guides to understanding children in general and do not necessarily apply to the individual child.

It is essential that the teacher have a comprehensive understanding of what the children do naturally in their graphic attempts in order to appreciate the child's developmental limitations, but a qualitative elementary art program that emphasizes the highest creative growth demands more of both teacher and student than what comes naturally. It is true, perhaps, that some children draw and compose intuitively with an innate feeling for interesting color, line, pattern, and special relationships, but the majority of

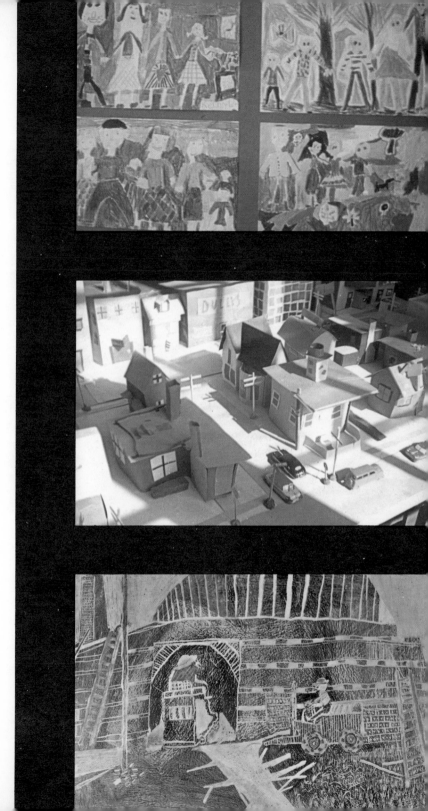

TOP—MY FAMILY, *crayon on manila paper (grade 2)*.
CENTER—*Group project. Construction paper (grade 4)*.
BOTTOM—*Multi-crayon engraving (grade 5)*.

The playground "jungle gym" creates an exciting design in space.

youngsters in our schools must be motivated, guided, and challenged towards greater design possibilities, fuller awareness of their environment, and richer aesthetic choices.

What do children really see? What can they be guided to see, to feel, and to perceive? Their parents and their teachers can widen children's horizons by helping them to respond to the thousand and one wonders around them:

Unusual cracks in old sidewalks and dried-up mud flats
Telephone wires that criss-cross against the sky
Subtle colors in winter snow
Grains in wood
Varied textures in the bark of trees
Space breakup and design of a jungle gym
Unusual textures in fabrics
Intricate design of a honeycomb
Face of the human race
Magnificent lines of bridges
Beauty of the ballet
Patterns of television antennas against the sky
Muted colors of early spring fields and farms
Many values and intensities of summer foliage
Different sizes and shapes in stone walls
Intriguing designs of peeled-off billboards and signs
Shadows of tree branches against a building
Subtle shapes and colors of driftwood and fall weeds
Unusual cornices of old buildings
Patterns of frost against a windowpane
Graceful movements of a cat
Golden shimmer of autumn haze
Overlapping ripples in a pond
Intricacy of a spider's web

Never-ending change of color orchestrations at dawn and
  sunset
Miracle of growing things
Filigree pattern in an insect's wings
Varied formations of clouds
Dew on early morning flowers and grass
Reflections in water
Neutralized colors of a foggy, rainy, or misty day
Flashing colors of stoplights, neon signs, and beacons
Highlights and sparkle in ocean waves
Unlimited shapes of pebbles and stones
Magic of sunlight filtering through a grille or screen
Luminosity of stained glass windows
Tracks of animals in the snow
Pattern of ivy against a wall
Endless variety of tree and leaf forms
Skeletal structure of animals
Patina on metal sculpture
Subtle color of moss on old stone work
Patterns of contoured farms from the air
Fiery smoke of foundry plants
Oil patterns on harbor waters
Shimmer of wheat fields in the wind

Learning to look intently is important for the young artist.

The child on his own is influenced daily by an environment which we as teachers cannot always control. Television, movies, billboards, store-window displays, magazine and album covers, newspapers, package designs, and advertisements, all shape his developing taste and affect his cultural quotient. What a qualitative art program can do, in some measure, is to help him to be more selective, more discriminating and more truly expressive in the many important choices he will make in his life.

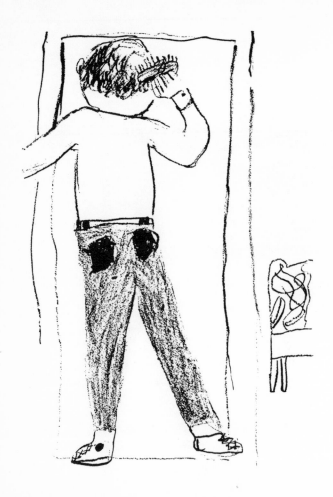

James, age eight.

Jean, age eight.

THE TEACHER'S ROLE

A creative, imaginative, sympathetic, and constantly resourceful teacher is *sine qua non* in the development and maintenance of a qualitative program in elementary art. The teacher of art should know the subject matter of his field and the characteristics of the children in his class, but in addition to this he must be an expeditious manager, housekeeper, resource planner, counselor, and budget expert. The successful art program is not built on one talent alone.

Without a competent and organized instructor at the helm, the art program may flounder and be submerged in a sea of last minute decisions, in trite and gimmicky patty-cake projects, and in chaotic, confused dead-ends. A sparkling physical plant, an un-limited materials budget, and a sympathetic administration are all laudable in the school program, but without a teacher of aesthetic sensibilities, convictions, and dedication of purpose, these may be just so many external assets without any contributing significance.

The reference to the teacher's dedication of purpose is deliberate. Dedication is and will always be a vital and militant force in our democratic educational pattern. It goes beyond skill, beyond competency, and beyond knowledge. It is predicated on a strong belief in the unique expressive potential of every child.

It is true you will find nothing in the teaching contract about dedication, not even in the small

print. Nor is there anything explicit in the agreement about the abstract endowments of love, patience, tact, and understanding that go hand in hand with good teaching. True dedication and involvement, whenever and wherever they occur, are in most cases freewill offerings on the part of the devoted teacher and cannot be measured except in the amount of inner satisfaction they bring the practitioner.

Every good teacher, whether special art teacher or classroom teacher of art, combines the qualities of competency and dedication. As a competent instructor, he has developed as broad a background as possible in the history and theory of art and can clarify for students the relationships between the contemporary and traditional forms in man's cultural heritage; he also performs in some area of arts and crafts to achieve personal aesthetic satisfaction; he understands the basic problems and techniques of the creative processes he teaches; he knows how to organize materials, tools, space, and time schedules to produce the best possible working conditions in the classroom; he is aware of the new and important findings in child psychology and mental therapy; and he bases the art program on the present needs and future demands of his students.

The dedicated art teacher enriches the lives of his students through daily experiences in some facet of art appreciation. In his enthusiasm, which he exhibits readily, he encourages his students to open their eyes to the design, color, form, rhythm, texture, and pattern in the world around them, in both natural

TOP—The teacher uses television to bring art to a wider audience. CENTER—Art gallery tours provide enrichment. BOTTOM—Teacher and student evaluate work at critical stages.

and man-made wonders; he identifies himself with his students; he does not always play it safe; he is excited and shows it when the student makes a discovery or masters a skill; he is concerned and genuinely perturbed when the student faces a problem.

The teacher-artist concept in education insures an art curriculum far above and beyond the normally accepted one. In a sense it guarantees a program of variety, scope, and individuality. The classroom teacher, sensitive to art and life around him, can move with confidence through planned aesthetic experiences toward a deeper and richer understanding of the arts. With this expanding knowledge he can make critical and justifiable evaluations of the students' work, build a classroom climate or atmosphere conducive to creative behavior, and continually experiment to develop ideas and processes that will help renew the children's interest in a project when necessary.

The wise art teacher plans the "question and answer" or discussion period explicitly and carefully. He does not leave this important part of the lesson to chance or "last minute" inspiration. Quite often he makes a written outline of his attack. Because the period allotted to art in so many of our schools is minimal, his questions are organized to bring out the richest reaction in the shortest time. As a rule his queries are the leading type, seldom calling for one specific answer. He proposes no blind-alley questions but presents those that open up new avenues and sometimes even suggest detours.

To keep quality high in the program, the best art teacher builds and keeps up to date as many available art resources as he can—slides, reproductions, photographs, films, curriculum guides, television kinescopes, tapes, illustrated books and magazine articles, research reports, and "technique" examples.

The competent art teacher develops self-confidence through constant practice in his field. He is prepared to present and expedite special art techniques in his class because he has experimented with them beforehand. He is continually on the alert for new ideas in the art world, new processes, new materials, new variations on common themes, and new ways of motivation. This research is necessary not only because of his students' needs but because of his own needs, his own revitalization as a creative person.

The discerning teacher of art learns to see the differences in every child's expression and builds on these unique differences. He discovers that no two children's interpretations of a subject will look exactly alike. In one the teacher will note a bold, spontaneous design approach; in another there will be a sensitive and delicate delineation; another may be concerned with the intricacy of pattern or texture; while another may reveal an imaginative and sparkling sense of color.

For the teacher of art, a positive, cheerful, animated, and sympathetic personality is a major asset. He should be genuinely interested in what the children are doing and learning; he must be patient, calm, and knowledgeable. Children want to believe that the teacher knows what he is doing. They come to rely on him for big decisions, or answers to perplexing problems, and for suggestions that help them get started. They are a bit skeptical of the teacher who confuses them with vague generalization and places all the responsibility in their hands, thus implying that he is uncertain himself.

The art teacher must learn to listen to the child's descriptions of his experiences and fantasies with sincere interest and sympathetic response. He should avoid playing the "poker face" with children. Instead, his excitement for the project, the process, or the children's ideas must show on his countenance, in his action, in his words, and in the sense of humor he displays. He should develop a well-modulated voice that can excite and create anticipation and enthusiasm and, when necessary, can project well enough to bring order and attentive response. The teacher who really *cares* about youngsters will not talk down to a child, and, most important of all, he will not underestimate the capabilities of any child at any age or his capacity to understand the wonderful challenge of art—its disciplines and its freedoms.

Perhaps the most harmful aspect of the current confusion of objectives in art education literature today is the position art teachers are forced to take in order to please everyone concerned. In too many instances we find art educators apologizing for making suggestions to children, for initiating projects, for influencing taste, and, quite frankly, for teaching art. In order to win approbation from both houses of the educational fraternity, such terms as "the children decided," "someone in class mentioned," "the class arrived at a solution" are commonly used in describing art projects. It is no secret that a knowledgeable teacher is definitely involved wherever a qualitative art program is in evidence. What is wrong with the teacher influencing, the teacher mentioning, and the teacher suggesting a solution?

As long as we insist on this "playing the middle ground" attitude in art education, we will have teachers with guilt complexes doing one thing and saying another. It is interesting to analyze some current writings in art education. In one paragraph the author will caution the teacher never to interfere with the child's expression and never to direct the project, yet in the very next paragraph he will say that a certain amount of guidance is necessary to help the child make a decision. What these writers are saying in effect is: "If I do it, it's guidance; if you do it, it's direction."

There is altogether too much unclarified controversy regarding how much *teaching* should be done— how much leading, guiding, challenging, directing, suggesting, planning, prompting, coaching, demonstrating, showing, criticizing, stimulating, pin-pointing, or motivating the art teacher should do. No wonder the classroom instructors today are in a quandary. Oddly enough, it is usually when teachers settle for what the child does naturally that no disagreement occurs, because then no real evaluation or definition of aesthetic criteria or quality is involved.

One of the most frequent questions asked at art education conventions and one that just as frequently goes unanswered is: "Just how much help should a teacher give a child?" One answer to this query, with a specific example of a project in process and four possible teaching approaches, is described here.

The second-grade youngsters (school and classroom nameless) are involved in drawing a live "cat and kittens" brought to class by one of their classmates. The teacher suggests that the children look carefully at the cat family and draw their reactions or impressions in crayon or chalk. The time allotted is approximately thirty minutes. Whatever the children do is accepted without evaluation or question, either because criticism might disturb or inhibit them or because the teacher does not feel confident enough to discuss their efforts pro or con.

Another teacher in another school, in another second grade, carries this project a step further. Before drawing begins, he plans a discussion period to talk about the cat and kittens, their relationships, their predominant characteristics, their movements, their color, their texture and shapes, and their environment. Children tell stories about their own cats. Nothing is said about composition per se and, as in the first approach, no further help or criticism is offered once the children begin drawing or painting.

Still another teacher, with a somewhat broader art background, helps the youngsters achieve a richer, more sensitive integration of experience and art,

Crayon drawings on colored construction paper (grade 2).

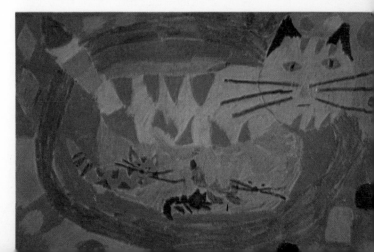

utilizing design and compositional factors. Like the second teacher he plans a motivating discussion, but he carries the challenge a bit further. He might say among other things: "Draw the cat and her family big enough to show us your idea. Try a light sketch first in a light color to see how all the family will fit in your picture. Plan your colors, your darks and lights, to emphasize the important parts. Practice some strokes of crayon or chalk on the back of your drawing to help you find the color or texture you want." The active role of this teacher ends here, and as in the case of the second teacher, the children are on their own during the studio period.

And finally, there is the teacher with strong convictions about the vital role of art awareness in the development of children who carries the function of guidance to its proper end. In addition to the pre-studio motivations, he moves about the classroom giving concrete suggestions when called upon, sensing design and compositional problems in cases where children need specific help, enthusiastically involving himself in the youngsters' discoveries, and evaluating their efforts at critical turning points.

The discerning teacher is aware, too, that the students in some instances do not fully appreciate or enjoy a new medium until they get fully involved in it. It is the art teacher's responsibility to provide the time and the necessary challenges for this involvement. Although one cannot arbitrarily impose a liking for a medium on a youngster, there are certain steps and procedures in introducing and developing a technique which might help build interest in the process.

If the procedure is completely alien to the children, the teacher with the cooperation of the class must at least demonstrate some basic approaches and developmental steps that the students can understand. He must also present the technical information in digestible segments and must repeat difficult steps when necessary.

It is often advisable to explore the specific tools or materials through trial experiments before tackling the final composition. The instructor, too, must know what the tools are capable of doing and must interpret this knowledge for his students. This does not negate the possibility of students discovering new uses for materials and tools. Exploitation of media should always be encouraged.

Even simple procedures that too often are taken for granted should be clearly explained. In the case of a multi-crayon engraving project, for example, the teacher would need to emphasize the kind of pressure needed and the probable sequence of color values necessary to insure a minimum of technical success. If presented in the right way, the students will find self-stimulation in the multi-color process, and new color relationships will be discovered, leading to deeper appreciations.

The subject matter and its adaptability to technique must be taken into consideration by the teacher. It might prove frustrating for the student to do a preliminary sketch in fine pencil and then lose this detailed and delicate interpretation in the bold and heavy strokes of a crayon or chalk composition.

The teacher must always be ready to help the student relate the sketch or drawing to the technique. For example, the utilization of a brush and India Ink or a felt nib marker as the primary sketching tool for a linoleum print is warranted because their boldness and directness have an affinity with the strong groove of the linoleum gouge. The many subtle ramifications that occur in printing with a linoleum block can often trigger the student into further exploration and experimentation. Encouraged by the teacher, the student may get involved in printing on acetate over color, on the colored section of discarded magazines, on newspapers, on colored tissue arrangements, on cloth, over colored ink experiments, on fingerpainted papers, or over ink-brayered surfaces.

The teacher, of course, is the prime catalyst and bridge builder. It is his responsibility to develop a climate of affection and permissiveness, of order and rationale, and of excitement and creativity. When a teacher really is concerned with the children in his class, he plans and does things the youngsters may not always approve of or enjoy. He may ask them to set higher criteria or standards of performance for themselves, or he may demand a little more effort from them than they have been accustomed to giving. He does this because he has a sincere conviction that whatever he challenges them to accomplish will enrich and enhance their lives today, as well as tomorrow.

Halli, age nine.

John, age nine.

AVENUES TO MOTIVATION

It is almost axiomatic that most children need some kind of stimulation or motivation to do their best art work. In every art education guide one reads, special reference is made to the fact that a youngster must have something to say before he can be inspired to say it.

Inspiration or stimulation for the youngster's art expression may come from his experiences at home, in the community, on the playground; from trips and from visits to museums, zoos, gardens, national parks, and monuments; or from movies, television, radio, books, magazines, and periodicals. The responsibility however, for reactivating these experiences and giving them an immediacy that will trigger the youngster into an art expression is the teacher's, and his alone.

He must be prepared to augment the child's store of knowledge and recall in order to emphasize the richer meanings and stronger identifications inherent in the experience. Specifically, he might ask the child the "How?" "What?" "Why?" or "Where?" regarding the event. This kind of questioning should be designed to encourage seeing and thinking, not just drawing. The important thing is the idea. The teacher must be able to help the children analyze the significant aspects of the experience. In many instances the teacher himself will have to provide the children with the motivating experiences through planned field trips and very often through vicarious means in the classroom itself. Because of this probability, he must have on hand or at close call a fund of audio-visual resources, such as slides or filmstrips of plant and animal forms, color reproductions, still-life material, mounted animals, pets, objects from nature such as rocks or dried plants, examples of particular techniques, illustrated magazine articles, recordings, and tapes.

The teacher, with this wealth of resource potential at his disposal and with an understanding of the capacity of the youngsters to react and perform, is better prepared to initiate art projects for the youngsters.

A good beginning sets the stage for the successful culmination of any art lesson. Projects initiated with objective planning, with experimentation by the teacher in the particular technique involved, with exciting and effective resources on hand, and with evaluative criteria used wisely, add immeasurably to the substance or continuity of the art program. The wise teacher must be able to envisage the entire project or process with all its accompanying problems. This does not mean that he will not be on the alert for any exciting innovations and developments that may occur during the project, but he must be continually aware of the possible aesthetic objectives.

Another vital factor in the planning of every project and especially crucial for the opening session is the housekeeping involved. The teacher must organize so that there will be adequate working space, a good supply of materials and tools, enough storage space for projects in progress and for those completed, effective cleanup facilities, convenient and easily accessible supply areas, and proper facilities for discussion, demonstration, and evaluation procedures.

Budgeting the time allowed for the art lesson is always an important consideration. The children must never feel that they are being rushed through any phase of the project. The good teacher carefully plans the amount of time needed for exchange of ideas, for demonstrations, for distribution and collection of materials, and for classroom cleanup.

The experienced teacher, as well as the novice, will find that by writing down the objectives for a new project, the varied goals to be reached by the youngsters are much more easily identified, and evaluations for the completed project can be more consistently defined. These objectives and criteria on the blackboard augment the teacher's effectiveness and are a constant reminder to the children, affording them the opportunity to make their own mental evaluations without continually consulting the busy teacher. Children in the primary grades will probably benefit more by having the teacher repeat the fundamental objectives of the project from time to time. Elementary art lessons are like pieces of a large puzzle, and each classroom lesson should bring the student closer to the solution of his particular creative problem.

Another important aspect that stimulates the discussion of ideas and experiences is an atmosphere or climate conducive to the development of creativity and sensitive awareness. The wise teacher allows the child to work independently until he sees that the child is in need of more challenges and more fuel. Only then does the teacher step in to help the child, urging him to go a little further, to move toward a new level of artistic growth. The good teacher uses different motivational approaches for different children. To do this sensitively and intelligently, he must have a diverse and comprehensive background in the arts and in child development.

The key to successful motivation is based on the subtle rapport which should develop between the teacher and his students. This kind of relationship may take a long time to develop, but once the teacher establishes a contact of respect and mutual understanding, his power to guide and to clarify ideas for the students becomes his high point of efficiency.

The knowledgeable teacher knows that some classes will need considerable motivation, while others may very often be self-motivated. The most vital introductory motivations that a teacher can make are structured on vivid and meaningful personal experiences. Nothing replaces actual perception or direct contact for intense stimulation. At all times and if at all possible the instructor should provide an immediate experience for the child to engage in, to feel, and to identify himself with.

Field trips to a museum, art gallery, farm, greenhouse, factory, fire station, or building site; guest visits by a doctor, nurse, policeman, astronaut, soldier, airman, sailor, lumberjack, fisherman, or athlete; and live animals or pets brought to class will provide stimulating and enthusiastic responses by the children.

In the classroom itself the teacher can display nature's ingenious forms—fruits, vegetables, seashells, seaweed, coral, driftwood, bark, insects, rock and mineral collections, live and dried plants, aquariums, stuffed birds, reptiles, fish, and mammals. Still-life objects such at bottles, lanterns, coffee grinders, bowls, coffee or teapots, vases, and a host of antique objects can be used with great success for elementary drawing projects.

At every opportunity the teacher should discourage the students' dependency on conventional design clichés and shorthand stereotypes. He should play down the "drawing-out-of-your-head" philosophy by emphasizing more drawing from things which can be

Interesting objects to draw can be found in many places.

touched, studied, explored, understood, and expressed.

Nature confronts us constantly with multiple components of art forms. In it we can see variety of line, color, value, and texture, as well as many design principles such as simplification, repetition, symmetrical and asymmetrical balance, emphasis, and unity. The teacher must lead the child back to nature. He must help him to see, to select, to analyze, to report, to edit, and to find in nature the parallel of art elements and art design. For instance, meaningful lines can help a child say many things. Curved lines define meandering creeks or rivers, circus tents, exits on expressways, cypress trees, insect bodies, people's faces, necks of birds, rolling waves, ridges, mountains, and valleys; radiating lines are found in the veins of leaves, tree branches and twigs, ferns, roots, and water ripples; and straight lines express soaring skyscrapers, telephone poles, television antennas, chimneys, water towers, fences, railroad tracks, construction girders, and airport beacons.

Only by encouraging the child to draw directly from nature can he really develop the careful, sensitive observation which can be the basis for a creative interpretation of the world around and about him. This direct and forthright experience becomes the catalyst for promoting a sound understanding of scientific knowledge, as well as an aesthetic comprehension of nature's forms. Thus beginning at the elementary level, the teacher is molding a personality capable of integrating both the scientific and aesthetic aspects into a unified and beneficial view of the world.

The teacher can help the child to look at nature in two ways: first, from a pragmatic point of view, for example, "This insect is a tiger swallowtail belonging to the group called Lepidoptera;" and secondly, from an aesthetic viewpoint, using his eyes like an artist to search out the fascinating and varying colors, texture, patterns, and line quality which are found in the butterfly's wing. This dual interpretation of the environment, of nature in her myriad aspects, should be encouraged in every art experience and expression.

Materials and tools used in art projects can be utilized also as motivating devices and in many cases are the main stimuli that fire the student's efforts. In the primary grades the introduction of new assortments of hues, both in crayon and tempera, brings added excitement to coloring. The free-flowing, inexpensive felt nib markers now available elicit an enthusiastic reaction from the youngsters. Tissue paper is now on the market in a host of bright colors that delight the primary child and help him discover new hues through overlapping.

In the intermediate grades the teacher can whet the artistic appetites of the students by introducing them to the use of scrap vinyl for mosaics, crayon for encaustic paintings, plaster of Paris for reliefs and carvings, reed and colored tissue for constructions, glazes and stains for patinas on sculpture, wax and dyes for batiks, metals for castings or repoussé reliefs, "found" objects for design impressions in clay, and acrylic polymer emulsions for new color experiments. There

A collection of arts and artifacts can enrich the school's art program.

has been some recent criticism regarding the introduction of so many new and diverse media and techniques in the school art programs. Some approaches may be questionable, but we believe that it is not so much the new materials themselves that are the source of trouble, as it is the manner in which the teachers and students exploit them that shocks the sensibilities. It is a known fact that one student with the best oil paints, canvas, and brushes may produce horrors, whereas another student may utilize discarded scraps from an attic or alley to create a thing of aesthetic merit.

The introductory lesson or session in an art project should be just as important as it is in other subject areas in school. It is unfair to the students to expect them to be challenged or excited by a series of projects or art lessons that begin simply with "draw this," or "draw that," or sometimes "just express yourself," or "paint what you want to today." The teacher of the art project should devote the same amount of time to the initial presentation of a unit as a teacher does in the preparation of the English or science units in his grade. There are many evocative ways to begin an art lesson. These include showing a film on the process, a filmstrip on the subject matter, or slides of examples by other students; guiding a discussion on related experiences; conducting a field trip to find objects that enrich the vicarious knowledge of the students; playing recordings to help set the mood for the creative act; demonstrating a process with student participation; introducing an exciting personality to

model for the class; or reading excerpts from stories, poems, or dramas. With this variety of motivational procedures, planned well in advance, the students can look forward to the art class as a unique and rewarding period of the school day. Each project, each process, each subject, demands its own kind of pattern of motivation, and only the teacher with a rich repertoire of ideas will be able to bring to the art program the spice it needs.

One of the most common problems the teacher of an art class faces is the lagging of student interest after the first excitement of a new project or lesson has worn thin. This is especially true of youngsters who do not set high standards for themselves and are satisfied with a superficial effort, or for those who do not have a real concern for, or identification with, the subject matter involved.

There are always some children in the art class who finish sooner than others or feel they have done as much as they can on a project while their classmates are still busily involved in their creations. This situation poses a real problem for the teacher because it involves a delicate balance between what the child can honestly accomplish in art with superior guidance, and what too often he is willing to settle for. If, at the outset of the lesson, the teacher, in collaboration with the students, could set up general goals and criteria to be achieved in technique, in composition, in structure, in color, and in texture, then the problem of the child who finishes quickly would not be such a critical one. These agreed-upon aesthetic criteria, posted on the blackboard or bulletin board, could be referred to when the children needed further stimulation or challenge. This procedure would also alleviate one of the major quandaries facing the classroom teacher, that of being able to guide each of his thirty or more students effectively and still manage the other varied chores of the classroom. When questions involving the project arise, the teacher could clarify them with the entire class as they work, rather than wasting time through constant repetition of objectives. Often projects in progress by class members could be shown with appropriate critical comment to emphasize the goals of the venture and to introduce possible variations. A clarification made in class to one student will often trigger ideas for other students who have reached an impasse or plateau.

At the upper elementary level the practice of writing brief constructive criticisms on slips of paper, attached to the student's artwork, is beneficial in a number of ways: it gives the teacher a chance to evaluate all the student's work at a time when he is not beset by other commitments; it insures the possibility that every student will receive help at critical stages; it clarifies for the student his specific problems; and it provides him with a working direction for the early part of the next class period that keeps him purposefully occupied while the teacher attends to those youngsters with special problems. This method, though it may appear tedious and time consuming to the busy teacher, helps him strengthen his evaluative

capacities and simultaneously gives purpose and seriousness to the art lesson.

Another more common method of renewing student interest through evaluation is to praise students' works which illustrate exciting composition, sensitive line, unique texture and pattern, unusual space delineation, or subtle or sparkling color relationships.

Because the child can only absorb or retain a few suggestions or ideas at one time, the teacher should plan to provide motivation in small doses. Introduce, if possible, a new and challenging stimulus each day. The following devices are suggested among many possibilities:

> *Reproductions* of paintings, sculpture, and prints that supplement and emphasize the objectives of the project;
> *Photographs* of the specific subject matter involved that will extend the students' experiences;
> *Color slides* of paintings, drawings, sculpture, prints, ceramics, jewelry, architecture, designs in nature and in the immediate everyday environment, creative works by other children illustrating technical stages in a process, and children, performers, and animals in action (this source of motivation should be continually augmented, since it enriches one of the most significant learning situations);
> *Filmstrips* on techniques, art history, and on correlated areas such as biology, anthropology, botany, geology, world geography, travel, space science, and technology;
> *Films, live TV shows,* and *kinescopes* that apply to a particular theme or technique;
> *Books* (stories, plays, poems, biographies), *periodicals,* and *pamphlets* that will broaden the knowledge of

both the teacher and student and bring richer interpretations of the subject matter;

Recordings (both disc and taped) of music, dramatizations, and of the varied sounds of different geographical regions, jungle animals, nature's forces, machines, rockets, trains, planes, ships, and circuses;

Radio programs of particular themes for classroom listening;

Guest speakers and *performers,* such as athletes, clowns, scuba divers, scientists, dancers, and astronauts;

Field and sketching trips to science and historical museums, art galleries, artists' studios, municipal buildings, farms, factories, wharves, airports, observatories, railroad yards, bus and transit terminals, historical sites, national parks, zoos, and shopping centers;

Models for classroom observation and drawing of live or stuffed birds, sea life, reptiles, mammals, pets, mounted insects, terrariums, ant colonies, bee hives, hobby collections, flowers and plant life, skeletons, and assorted still-life material—fruit, vegetables, lanterns, kettles, pots, vases, bottles, kitchen utensils, trivets, and textural cloths like fish net or burlap;

Artifacts from other cultures, such as masks, carvings, jewelry, textiles, ceramics, toys, tools, icons, and fetishes;

Examples of work in various media by former students;

Demonstrations by teacher and students;

Constructive critiques by class members with positive guidance by the teacher;

Introduction of a new material or tool, a new use for common material, or a new way of using a tool;

Introduction of a design principle or a special emphasis on some compositional element, such as value, texture, or color relationship;

Exhibits and *bulletin board displays* that relate to the unit;

Use of microscopes, magnifying glasses, telescopes, and *microscopic projectors* to expand visual horizons.

A specific example of the utilization and exploitation of this day-to-day renewal of interest is illustrated in the following project of *toothpick-reed-applicator stick construction* for upper-grade youngsters.

The first class period could be devoted to an introduction of the basic material to the class. Small pieces of reed and other similar materials might be passed around to the students, described as to their source, and discussed in general terms with emphasis on the specific qualities of the material. In this initial meeting, too, the teacher could monitor a discussion on subject matter possibilities, including insects, birds, fish, mammals, and constructions of the future.

The second class session might be applied to sketching the object to be constructed, using either the stuffed mammal exhibits of a local museum; resources such as films, slides, or photographs; or recalled experiences. (To carry out our analysis let us assume that some form of animal life is chosen as the subject matter for the project.) During the sketching session the teacher might stress capturing the significant form of the animal and the exploitation of design and detail. He might also emphasize simplification of the basic form without losing the characteristic qualities of the animal, delineation of the curvilinear aspects that lend themselves to the inherent qualities of the material, and stress on the significant features of the animal, like the beak and eyes of a bird, the gill of a fish, the

antennae of an insect, or the horns on a rhinoceros. Line sketches could be executed in pencil, black crayon, or the new felt nib markers which facilitate a free-flowing contour line.

The third lesson could be devoted to the construction of the fundamental toothpick-reed-applicator stick forms. The session might begin with the teacher demonstrating the bending and forming of the pre-soaked reed to create the basic forms. After attaching the drawing securely to a similar size piece of corrugated cardboard or Celotex, the instructor might show the students how to pin the wet reed to conform to their sketch, criss-crossing the pins on both sides of the reed to keep it from springing out of shape.

The teacher might start the fourth class period by acquainting the students with the special type of adhesive necessary to hold these constructions together, in this case Testor's Formula AA extra-fast-drying airplane cement. A demonstration of the proper application of the glue could be made with a cautious reminder that the reed must be dry before the glue will adhere properly. At this session several possible structural variations could be suggested which would allow for individual preferences and interpretations. The amount of time needed for this phase of the construction will vary with different age levels and capabilities. When most of the students have completed their basic form in characteristic terms, the teacher could take the next and final motivational step. This would be the introduction of the many possible affinitive materials that could be used

Steps in reed construction (grade 6).

to give emphasis, color, contrast, and individuality to each project completed. Among these are corks and sheet cork, string, cardboard, bamboo scraps, balsa wood, colored tissue, colored construction paper, wooden beads, and subtle one-color cloth remnants.

Timing is of the utmost importance in motivation. The teacher should be able to sense when the children have reached a dead-end and need stronger incentives to make progress in their work. The initial part of the class period is usually the best time to introduce new ideas because the youngsters are most receptive then. The teacher should not interrupt a busily working class to present a point that could have been made at the outset of the period. Motivations should be psychologically budgeted so that the youngsters will not feel cheated out of their working period. The teacher will learn in time to gauge the listening and interest span of the students and plan the motivation-discussion-demonstration segments realistically and profitably.

Finally, it is important to remember that every creative unit is but one small part of the whole, and that a successfully concluded project is the best possible motivation for the next adventure in art.

MOTIVATIONAL RESOURCES

A creative teacher will find many occasions to exploit the following motivational resources in the art program:

Acetate or celluloid sheets of varied colors
An aquarium of tropical fish
Ant farm
Bells from the Far East
Chinese ivory carvings
Driftwood, tumbleweed, cornstalks
Duck decoys
Eskimo sculpture
Fish netting
Growing plants of all kinds
Indian ceremonial headdress
Indian corn, hedge apples
Insect, rock, and stamp collections
Japanese paper fish kite
Japanese scrolls and wood-block prints
Kachina or Kokeshi dolls
Magnifying glass
Mannequins (display)
Masks: African, Japanese no, Mexican, Mardi gras, Northwest Pacific Indian, theatrical, clown
Mexican pottery
Model cars and train engines
Musical instruments
Navaho Indian rugs
Old-fashioned hats
Old spinning wheels, lanterns, and lamps
Paper cut-outs from Poland
Peruvian or Guatemalan textiles
Plastic plants and leaves
Puppets from far-off countries
Spanish-Mexican Santos
Sports equipment
Spotlights
Swedish colored glass
Tape recorder
Texture table
Theatrical make-up and costumes
Tropical birds in a cage

Kathy, age ten.

John, age ten.

5

PLANNING
A PROGRAM

A well-planned sequence of creative projects, based upon the teacher's developed aesthetic convictions and on his understanding of the child's interests, needs, and expressive potential, is the core and foundation of a qualitative program in art.

The effective art curriculum is structured around the life experiences of the children, their interest in nature, in hobbies, in games and sports, in holidays, in travel, in family and friends, and in the many activities centered around the school. Instead of following a nebulous, will-o'-the-wisp pattern on the assumption that elementary art has no real substance to offer, the program should provide a strong continuity of learning with a high aesthetic caliber. In

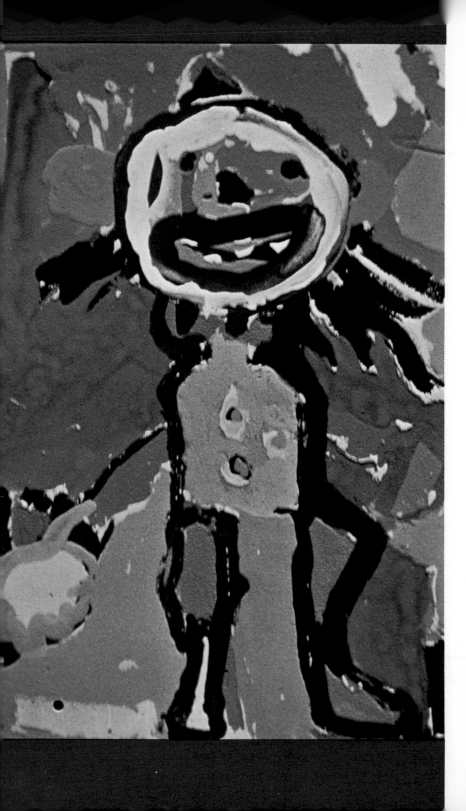

too many cases projects are based on hastily concocted motivations with superficial and chaotic results. A qualitative program in art must provide a variety of challenges in a wide range of exciting materials; it must allow for art sessions long enough for real involvement in a problem or technique; it must present new and worthwhile experiences and occasions for self-discovery; and it must provide the child with many opportunities to explore, experiment, select, organize, and appreciate.

One of the most important roles a teacher can play in the development of a high-standard art program is to ensure the continuity of aesthetic and expressive growth. In order to do this effectively, he must know what children can accomplish in art at various age levels and must be able to identify the particular art goals for the grade he teaches. Repetition is, of course, highly necessary for learning, but the same gimmick foisted on the children from grade to grade, year after year, leads to frustration and boredom. The introduction of basic art concepts, new techniques and processes, and new tools at different maturation levels will provide scope, direction, and meaning to the art curriculum. Either through consultation with the art supervisor or on his own, the classroom teacher should make a real effort to meet with other teachers in the school and plan a developmental art program. This might be done during preschool orientation week.

The instructor will discover that certain art fundamentals and concepts emphasized from grade to grade

Tempera painting on manila paper (grade 1).

are retained by the students and make the task of teaching easier in later, more complex, projects. Youngsters who learn about color relationships, patterns, and space-filling shapes in grades one and two often recall aspects of this knowledge when it is reinforced in grades three and four, until it finally becomes a definite part of their interpretative repertoire.

Effective curriculum planning must be preceded by identification and clarification of the art objectives or goals for each age level. These criteria usually spell the difference between a mediocre, adequate, above average, or qualitative program. The teacher, bolstered with a knowledge of what the child does naturally, will be able to utilize art disciplines and resources to help the child express his ideas in a more effective, more orderly, and more artistic idiom. All techniques, processes, elements, and principles of design, if introduced gradually and at the child's level of understanding, make the art period more rewarding and provide a foundation for future art growth.

The child in first and second grades should be guided and encouraged to utilize his material to its fullest degree, whether it be filling the page with a drawing, pressing on the crayon to create a rich surface, or exploring the many possibilities of paint and brush. He should be guided to identify basic colors, to repeat colors to achieve the singular effects he desires, to recognize simple values and intensity of colors, and to distinguish and make use of contrasting colors in his compositions. Through planned motivation via assorted excursions into sensitivity and aware-

TOP—Crayon drawing on colored construction paper (grade 1). CENTER—Chalk drawing on colored construction paper (grade 1). BOTTOM—Colored construction paper picture (grade 1).

ness, the teacher should help the child become conscious of texture and pattern in nature and art.

Subtle admonitions, queries, and suggestions like: "Fill the space," "That's a fine start—all different shapes!" Let the paint flow," "Make your brush dance," "Make your biggest shapes first," "Think with your crayon," "Something big, something small, something short, something tall — something dark, something bright, helps to make your work all right," prove purposeful in helping the young child at critical moments.

This kind of evaluative comment can be augmented at the second-grade level with: "What new colors have you discovered?" "How many colors of green can you use in your painting?" "How many different patterns have you used in your design?"

The third and fourth grade child is learning to take directions and criticism in his stride. He is aware of his graphic limitations and often seeks the teacher's help. Basically he should learn to recognize and use an expanded range of colors, including tints and shades, to mix secondary and intermediate colors, to identify or distinguish related warm and cool colors, to utilize emphasis and rhythm, and to understand the variations of symmetrical and asymmetrical balance.

The teacher must facilitate the child's comprehension of the various possibilities of rhythm through repetition of a key color, significant shape, dominant movement, specific line, and characteristic texture. The pupil can learn to create unity, too, through over-

38

TOP—Colored chalk drawing on colored construction paper (grade 1). CENTER—Painting done with black crayon and watercolors (grade 1). BOTTOM—Painting done with felt nib markers and watercolors (grade 1).

lapping of shapes and colors, through specific color relationships, especially limited color ranges, and through the use of affinitive materials.

Children in the fifth and sixth grades can be persuaded to plan their pictures more carefully in terms of developed composition and design. They can be motivated to acquire a vocabulary of art terms through actual use and discussion and taught to study and appreciate the works of distinguished artists and craftsmen. All their understandings now take on a more complex nature as they build and maintain an inquiring, experimental attitude.

Increased discrimination leads them to use new and more subtle color combinations, to exploit the mixed media of crayon and watercolor, tempera and ink, paper and wire, chalk and yarn, and to try combination of collage, drawing, and painting.

They are now ready to tackle more unique space relationships, to solve specific problems of distance through one- or two-point perspective, to manipulate intricate tools and devices in printmaking, metalwork, repoussé reliefs, mosaic, reed constructions, ceramics, and sculpture.

At this level, too, they can learn to identify the tertiary or intermediate colors. Complementary, analogous, and triad color combinations can be discussed, but not as definitive solutions to color problems.

More specific suggestions for the teacher at all levels of instruction and for all techniques will be found in Chapter 6.

TOP—Self-portraits done with tempera paint (grade 1). CENTER—Painting done with a felt nib marker and watercolors (grade 1). BOTTOM—Basic cone shape constructed of paper (grade 1).

39

The most stimulating programs take place where the teacher is willing to try something new and challenging. He must always be alert for new materials or for commonplace materials that can be used in subtle and aesthetic ways.

To aid the teacher in expediting program planning, the art projects for the various grades might be divided into the following general categories: drawing and painting, constructing, printmaking, carving (sculpture), cutting and pasting (collage), modeling, and mixed-media experiences.

The teacher will find that the subject matter of visual expression is basically the same for all grade levels. It consists generally of people, places, events, and things in the child's environment, plus the exciting and unique embodiments of the youngster's imagination. The interpretation of these experiences and the child's technical dexterity will change and expand as the child grows.

The teacher must plan for the continuous development of a process or technique as the youngster progresses from grade to grade. The introduction of developed aesthetic concepts, new tools and materials, and more complex processes will give scope, direction, and integrity to the art program.

Although the majority of projects suggested here are usually interpreted on an individual basis, many of them can be developed as group projects, depending on the teacher and on the cooperative ability of the children.

TOP—Tempera painting (grade 2). CENTER—Crayon and chalk drawing on gray manila (grade 2). BOTTOM—Tempera painting on colored construction paper; one of a series of masks for a group totem pole (grade 2).

SUGGESTED PROJECTS IN ART

CONTENT	TECHNIQUE OR MEDIA

DRAWING AND PAINTING

The Child

Playing with My Friends	Crayon on colored construction paper
Picking Flowers in the Garden	Crayon-watercolor resist on white drawing paper
My Pet and I	Tempera paint on chipboard, bogus, or gray manila paper
Fun in the Snow	White and colored crayon or chalk on dark construction paper

His Family, His Home

On a Picnic	Black crayon line and tempera on assorted papers
At the Park	Crayon-watercolor resist on white drawing paper
At the Supermarket	Colored chalk or Crayons on colored construction paper
The House I Live in	Colored crayon on colored construction paper

His Other Interests

A Trip to a Farm	Crayon on colored construction paper
Santa's Workshop	Mural: tempera on oak tag, kraft paper, chipboard, or on construction paper, 36-inch-wide roll
The Vegetable Market	Mural: colored chalk on kraft paper or colored construction paper, 36-inch-wide roll
Animals in the Zoo	Felt nib markers on manila paper, colored construction paper, or sheets from wallpaper sample books
Butterflies or Birds	Mobile: tempera on cardboard, painted on both sides and cut out

MODELING

Animals on the Farm	Clay, individual or group project
On the Playground	
Animals of the Jungle	

CONSTRUCTING

| Imaginary Animals or People | Construction, paper sculpture |
| Easter Bunnies | Assorted found materials, cloth remnants |

CUTTING AND PASTING (collage)

Land of Make-Believe	Colored poster and construction paper
People from Another World	Colored sections from discarded magazines
Birds in a Cage	Colored construction paper and yarn

DRAWING AND PAINTING
The Child in Action

Skating on the Rink or River or Lake	Tempera on bogus, chipboard, Muraltex, or gray manila
Playing Ball	Colored crayon on colored construction paper
Skipping Rope; On the Jungle Gym	Black crayon, felt nib markers, and watercolor
Skiing, Sledding, and Tobogganing	Colored chalk on colored construction paper
Fun at the Swimming Pool	Tempera on oak tag, bogus, colored construction paper, or Muraltex

His Family, His Home

Washing the Family Car	Crayon on manila or colored construction paper
Spring Cleaning	Colored chalk on colored construction paper

Community Interests

Community Helpers (see list at end of this chapter)	Crayon or tempera on colored construction paper

Other Interests

Bugs and Beetles	Colored chalk on colored construction paper
Things on a Table (still life)	Crayon on dark-colored construction paper
Fifty Fathoms Deep (Fish in the Sea)	Mobile: tempera on cardboard, painted on both sides and cut out
Tree of Life	Crayon-watercolor resist on white drawing paper
All about Indians	Tempera on Muraltex or colored construction paper
Flowers in a Garden	Multi-crayon engraving on oak tag

MODELING

Noah's Ark	Earth clay; group project

PRINTMAKING

Allover Design	Vegetable (potato) print

CONSTRUCTING

Totem Poles	Tempera on colored construction paper
Flu Bugs	Paper sculpture
Space Vehicles	Box sculpture

CUTTING AND PASTING (collage)

Autumn Trees	Colored poster and construction paper
Animals in the Jungle	Mural: colored construction paper on Upson board, or on 36-inch-wide construction paper roll

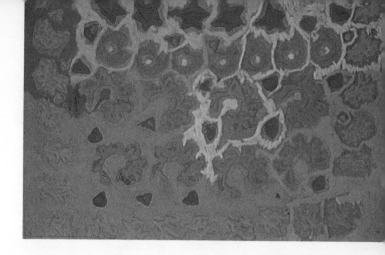

TOP LEFT—*Tempera painting on Muraltex paper (grade 3).*
CENTER LEFT—*Crayon engraving (grade 3).* TOP
RIGHT—*Vegetable print using tempera paint and chalk on
colored construction paper (grade 2).* CENTER RIGHT—
*Colored chalk drawing on colored construction paper (grade
2).* BOTTOM—*Crayon drawing on colored construction
paper (grade 2).*

TOP—Stabile made with applicator sticks and colored construction paper (grade 3). CENTER—Mobile fish made with tempera paint on heavy butcher paper, stuffed with newspapers, and stapled (grade 3). BOTTOM—Felt-nib-marker drawing with a colored tissue overlay (grade 3).

DRAWING AND PAINTING
Around the Town
Traffic Jam	Felt nib marker or black crayon and watercolor on white drawing paper
Boarding the Bus	Crayon on colored construction paper
At the Airport	Crayon-watercolor resist on cream or white paper
Window Shopping	Tempera on colored construction paper
Four-Alarm Fire	Crayon engraving on white drawing paper or oak tag

Visits and Travel
A Train Trip	Chalk on colored construction paper
A View from a Helicopter	Multi-crayon engraving on oak tag
A Visit to a Museum	Felt nib markers and watercolor on white drawing paper

Other Interests
The Animal Kingdom	Pencil or felt nib marker on gray manila
Rare Birds	Colored chalk on black or deep-colored construction paper
Clowns	Tempera on gray manila or Muraltex board
Circus Train	Mural frieze: tempera on oak tag, cardboard, or colored construction paper roll

MODELING
Circus Animals	Clay
Ceramic Pots	Clay, coil or slab method

CONSTRUCTING
Tropical Fish	Mobile: tempera on kraft paper; two sides of fish stapled together and stuffed with shredded newspaper
Abstract Stabiles	Reed, toothpicks, corks, wooden beads, applicator sticks, balsa strips, colored construction paper, cardboard

CUTTING AND PASTING (collage)
Discoveries	Form colored tissue shapes on white drawing paper
Insect World	Colored poster and construction paper
Flower Garden	Mosaic with colored construction paper or colored sections of book jackets

PRINTMAKING
Allover Designs	Tempera and India ink batik on colored construction paper
Animal Kingdom	Cardboard prints

GRADE FOUR

DRAWING AND PAINTING

Themes of Action

Bicycle (go-cart) Races	Colored felt nib markers on newsprint, manila, or colored construction paper
Flying Kites	Mural: Sketcho on Muraltex board or thin Upson board
Tug of War	Black crayon and watercolor on white drawing paper
Climbing a Tree (Tree House)	Crayon-watercolor resist on white drawing paper
Games and Sports	Assorted media
Drawing the Figure	Pencil, felt nib marker, charcoal stick, stick and ink
From memory	
From a posed model	
Self-Portraits with Musical Instruments	Tempera or Sketcho on Muraltex board, gray manila, or bogus

Other Interests

Dancers of the World	Tempera, Sketcho, or colored chalk
Spiders and Their Webs	Crayon engraving
The World of Butterflies	Crayon-watercolor resist

MODELING

Birds	Clay reliefs, fired and glazed
Fish Motifs	Clay jewelry

CONSTRUCTING

Performers	Wire sculpture
Birds on a Tree	Plaster of Paris gauze (Paris craft)

PRINTMAKING

Cityscape	Plaster relief print
Musical Instruments	Cardboard or linoleum print

CARVING (sculpture)

Fish Forms	Plaster of Paris and vermiculite mix in milk-carton mold

CUTTING AND PASTING (collage)

Still Life	Colored poster, construction paper, and wallpaper samples
Landscape	

MIXED MEDIA

Imaginary Worlds	Plaster reliefs from clay negative molded in a shallow shoe box
Fish, Birds, and Animals	

LEFT—Drawings done with colored felt nib markers on white drawing paper (grade 4) depicting Seattle World's Fair scene shown in the center. TOP RIGHT—Crayon-watercolor resist (grade 4). CENTER RIGHT—Tempera painting on colored construction paper (grade 4). BOTTOM RIGHT—Crayon engraving (grade 4).

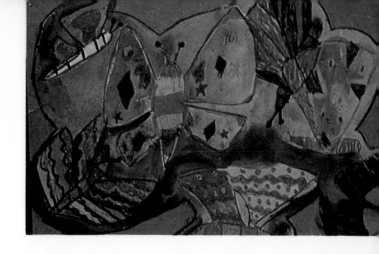

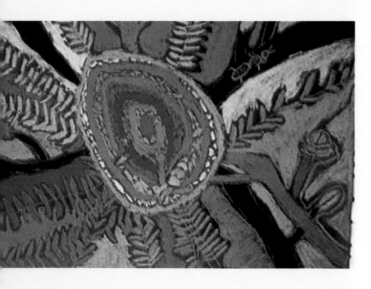

*TOP LEFT—*OUTER SPACE, *a group mural (4' x 8') on Upson board (grade 5). CENTER LEFT—Colored-chalk drawing on black construction paper (grade 5). BOTTOM LEFT— Design using colored chalk on colored construction paper combined with tempera spatter over leaves (grade 5).*

48

DRAWING AND PAINTING

Expanding Horizons

Worlds of Outer Space   Tempera, Sketcho, chalk, multi-crayon, or colored felt nib markers on assorted
The Radiation Belts   papers
Space Probe
The Sea Below

The Sporting World

The Ice Carnival   Same media and techniques as listed above
Archery Contest
The Tennis Match
Sports' Car Races
Water Sports

Other Interests

Plant Forms (Terrarium)   Multi-crayon engraving
Self-Portraits   Monoprints
Insect World   Tempera-India ink batik

MODELING

Birds   Clay reliefs with incised designs on the surface
Prehistoric Animals   Clay with surface designs made with "found" objects

CONSTRUCTING

Masks   Plaster of Paris gauze over simple bowl forms
Birds, Insects, and Fish   Vinyl plastic mosaic on masonite or plywood

PRINTMAKING

Leaf Abstractions   Colored chalk on colored construction paper
                                 Leaf stencils

Animals in Their Habitats   Linoleum block print

CARVING (sculpture)

Animals in Repose   Plaster of Paris or cement mix mold
Mask Forms, Nonobjective Forms   Jewelry from plaster of Paris spoon mold

DRAWING AND PAINTING

Figure Drawing from Posed Model — Ball point pen, Conté crayon, charcoal, pen and ink, bamboo pen, pencil

Figure Compositions

Outdoor Sketches — Chalk, felt nib pen, Sketcho, Craypas

Self-Portraits

Landscape or Cityscape — Crayon engraving or tempera batik on oak tag or Muraltex board

Still Life — Tempera batik, watercolor, or crayons

Rare Birds or Fish — Melted crayon on gesso-coated masonite or heavy cardboard; apply with Q-tips

CERAMICS

Pots — Clay, slab method

CONSTRUCTING

Fish or Insects — Reed, balsa wood, colored cardboard

Nonobjective Forms such as Playground Equipment or Homes of the Future — Applicator sticks, toothpicks, string, colored tissue, paste sticks, airplane glue, colored cord

PRINTMAKING

Portraits or Landscapes — Celluloid engraving (discarded X-ray plates, cleaned with laundry bleach)

The Animal World — Monoprints on colored construction paper

The Plant World

CARVING

Animals in Repose — Plaster of Paris or cement mixture

Birds or Fish — Driftwood, firebrick, Featherock, sculpturing wax

CUTTING AND PASTING (collage)

Alley Scenes, Harbors, Bridges, Construction Sites, Farm Buildings — "Found" materials on cardboard or masonite (see Appendix E)

MISCELLANEA AND MIXED MEDIA

Metal Enameling, Metal Casting

Etched Aluminum Jewelry

Repoussé Reliefs in Aluminum or Copper

COMMUNITY HELPERS

Nurse
Doctor
Milkman
Professor
Truck driver
Construction worker
Conductor
Minister
Baker
Judge
Farmer
Ferry operator
Pilot
Gardener
Lifeguard
Librarian
Auto mechanic
Toll collectors
TV repairman
Zoo keeper
Beautician
Chef
Pharmacist
Teacher

Postman
Fireman
Telephone lineman
Policeman
Dentist
Train Engineer
Sanitation Engineer
Grocer
Lawyer
Ambulance driver
Ship's captain
Bus driver
Stewardess
Forest ranger
Carpenter
Gas station attendant
Wrecker operator
Telephone operator
Chemist
Artist
Office secretary
Newspaper editor
Highway patrolman
Musician

COMMUNITY HELPERS, *crayon drawings (grade 2).*

Sue, age eleven.

Rory, age eleven.

6

A PROGRAM
IN ACTION

A representative number of projects and techniques fundamental to the repertoire of the elementary school art program are described in detailed terms on the following pages. They include both two- and three-dimensional activities. Though there may be some disagreement with the merits of the unit approach, we have found that classroom teachers are very often in the dark about the commonest and simplest processes in painting, printmaking, collage, sculpture, and crafts. They know a great deal about the child, his behavior, and his characteristics, but they know too little about the many procedures they must follow to help him specifically in art.

These capsule descriptions of art projects in action deal with both the practical and theoretical aspects of the lesson. They suggest motivational possibilities, clarify complex techniques, and specify aesthetic criteria. In no instance is the implication intended that these are the only approaches or interpretations possible, but for the record they have been researched, tested, and evaluated in a typically crowded elementary art class filled with eager, bright, slow, quiet, fidgety, sleepy, tired, energetic, noisy, inquisitive, and wonderful children. The illustrations of the projects speak for themselves.

Black crayon drawing (grade 2).

DRAWING THE FIGURE

What should the teacher say to the child about drawing the human figure? When should he say it? How much should he say? Is there a place in the elementary art program for drawing the figure per se? When should proportion in figure drawing be introduced? What methods of drawing the figure should be exploited? These are some of the pertinent questions that the teacher must resolve if the art program is to function as a valid part of the school's complex curriculum.

The most common advice offered to classroom teachers apropos figure drawing is, "Let the child alone—he will find his own way." This might be a comforting thought to the troubled teacher but one seldom recommended in any other subject area where learning takes place. If we want the child to grow in use of the human figure, we must provide steps to growth.

There are some things the teacher can do to help children with figure drawing. Youngsters can learn a great deal from the posed model in any grade. If children in the first or second grade draw the figure in their pictures, they have, one presumes, observed it at some time to enable them to put down their impressions of it. The interpretation of the figure in children's work, even in the primary grades, does not emerge out of a vacuum. What is wrong then with the closer observation, the more immediate perception, and the more definite awareness that the use of a posed figure in class offers?

Before the drawing starts the teacher can discuss the human figure. He can ask deliberate, leading, and discerning questions about the student who is posing. "What *kind of action* is the model performing? What parts of the model's body do you see, Mary? Jim, do you see what Mary sees? What do you think is the most important part of the model, Mike? How would you make it important? How big are the hands? The model is holding a bat. Could he hold it well if his hands were small? Put your hand over your face. Did you realize your hands were that big? How are the head and the shoulders joined together? How are the legs attached to the body?"

"Sometimes we look but we really do not see. What else can we use to see with besides our eyes? Now, as we look at the model, let us feel how our own arms go into our body. How large are they where they join? Where are they the thinnest? How big must our feet be to keep us steady on the ground? Where do our bodies bend? Where do our arms bend? Where do our legs bend? Where do our fingers reach when our arms are at our sides? How high can we reach over our head? How far can we swing around? How far can we bend backwards?"

"Before we begin, let us look at the model once more. Let us get our eyes full of the person we are drawing. Some very important things to remember are that *we should not rush; we should not make lazy or hasty lines; we should look first, then draw.* If we make our figure large enough to fill the page, all our classmates will be able to enjoy it, even from across the room. Everyone's drawing of the model will be different because we are all different, but if we want to tell others what we see and feel, we must first really see and really feel it ourselves."

Figure drawing teaches the child to be observant. It is amazing how quickly the growing, sensitive child sees characteristic details such as belts, shoelaces, ties, hair ribbons, necklaces, bracelets, pockets, buttons, ruffles, pleats, or the pattern in clothes, such as flowers, stripes, plaids, and diamonds, using them to enrich his interpretation of the figure he draws.

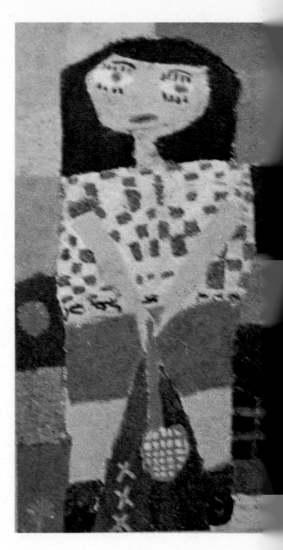

Sketcho (oil-base crayon) drawing on Muraltex board (grade 4).

It is important that figure-drawing experiences in the intermediate grades lead to some planned utilization of the figure in a painting, mural, print, or wire sculpture. Of course, the sketched figure can be developed as a composition in itself when the subject matter involves only one person in an activity such as: *I am playing ball, I am riding a bike.*

In the uncharted sea of figure drawing most classroom teachers are somewhat unsure of themselves and so settle for what the child can do on his own without any interference on their part. They conclude, because they themselves lack confidence in their own figure-drawing ability, that it would be presumptuous for them to make suggestions to the child. But what about the growing youngster himself? Shouldn't he get as much guidance in this crucial activity as he gets in mathematics, in English, or in science? We do not suggest stereotyped or rigid formulas, such as stick or sausage tricks, proportions measured to the half inch, or other conforming devices, but we strongly believe that there should be a correlation of empathic, perceptive, and aesthetic objectives in the presentation of figure-drawing experiences. We have suggested some basic approaches for the primary youngster. Now we offer the teacher some motivational and developmental possibilities for upper-grade children.

> Plan the figure-drawing event as a unique occasion to challenge the inquisitive and exploratory nature of the students.
>
> Make the introduction of each lesson stimulating and visually effective.

TOP—Children express action with an economy of line (grade 2). BOTTOM—The child's world includes his pets (grade 2).

Have someone model in a colorful costume or sports attire.

Introduce new drawing tools such as the free-flowing felt markers, ball point pens, or sticks and India ink.

Pose the model against a contrasting sheet of cardboard or Upson board that is slightly larger than the model himself. This will help the youngster see the figure filling a definite or positive space. The board, too, might indicate the boundaries of his drawing paper.

Demonstrate a new approach to drawing the figure: contour, gesture, mass, scribble. In blind contour drawing the student looks only at the model as he draws, never at his paper, except to locate another starting point. The teacher must insist on this procedure if the student is to achieve a true contour drawing.

Try a dual pose or a trio in a pose. Pose the model in a composition with a still life.

Let the students use their imaginations in drawing the figure. Allow the action or pose of the figure to trigger a theme or idea for them.

Suggest that the students take the pose of the model for a few seconds to get the feel of the action.

Vary the pose so that the students are not always presented with the same view.

Have the model present an action in sequence such as three steps in picking up a ball. Suggest the overlapping of the three successive poses in three different colors of crayon.

Vary the size of the paper the children draw on. Try some long thin 12- by 24-inch sheets for standing poses —some square sheets for crouching poses. If you have room in your class, be sure to give the children a

Youngsters draw best what they know best (grade 2).

58

chance to work on large sheets (24 by 36 inches) of paper with big brushes or felt nib markers.

Introduce different kinds of paper to draw on: news-print, cream or gray manila, white drawing, brown kraft or butcher, colored construction, Muraltex, bogus, or classified ad pages from the daily paper.

Don't forget the cut-paper approach to figure interpretation either by drawing first and cutting, or by using the contour method of looking at the model and cutting simultaneously.

There may be a skeleton in someone's closet—most likely the science department's—if so beg or borrow it, and you can really get down to fundamentals in figure drawing. Children in the fifth and sixth grade could benefit from an analysis of the bone structure when they face problems in drawing joints of the body.

If possible, use lightweight Upson or beaverboard drawing boards that the students can tilt against their desks or tables. This gives them a better working position in which they can see the model and their drawing surface with ease.

For action or gesture drawings which require a freer approach than the contour method, the teacher might suggest that the youngsters hold the crayon or pencil not like a writing tool but on its side like a drawing or sketching tool.

Encourage identification with self through dramatizations of activities that have meaning for the youngsters— playing a musical instrument, picking flowers, riding a bicycle, performing a dance, playing football, basketball, or baseball, standing under an umbrella in the rain, diving into a pool, hunting with a dog, balancing on a fence, modeling in a fashion show, skipping rope, or jumping on a trampoline.

Pen and ink contour drawings from models (grade 6).

Cityscape drawn with black crayon and white chalk on gray manila paper (grade 6).

DRAWING THE LANDSCAPE

Children in the upper grades react positively and effectively to their expanding environment. Whereas young children in the primary grades enjoy drawing single objects—a house, a tree, a flower, or an animal —the growing child responds to the challenge of the whole landscape and the "interrelation of parts." He is interested in outdoor sketching and the excitement of a field trip. The busy world unfolds at his very doorstep—the construction down the street, the perspective down an alley, the busy shopping center, the big city skyscrapers, the fairgrounds, the cluster of farm buildings, the rock-bordered ocean, the vista of mountain and ranch, the village park and band-shell, the soaring churches and synagogues, the factory, the beautiful bridges, the service station, the bus and train terminals, the school and the playground, the boat marinas and locks on the river, the harbor and the ships, the airport, the city of the future, or the everyday commonplace view from a bedroom window—these sights and many more can become the inspiration for his compositions and paintings. A variety of media can be used for outdoor sketches: pencil, charcoal, felt nib markers in black or in color, pen or stick and India ink, or black crayon.

Some youngsters sketch with confidence when on field trips, but many of them pose a recurring question for the teacher: "Where or how do I begin?" "What should I draw first?" Sometimes the complex view overwhelms them—sometimes the space problem confuses them. There are one or two approaches to landscape or cityscape drawing that might be suggested. In one instance the teacher might recommend that the child begin with a light sketch to establish his planes and basic shapes, one that could be easily changed when the necessity arose. Soft vine charcoal or pencil is usually best for this kind of searching sketch. Once the youngster has established his impression, he can develop the darker values and details.

Another technique that works for many children, especially when the view is complex and busy, is to suggest that the child find something in the center of the view that attracts him—a doorway, a telephone pole, an outdoor stairway, a window, a tree, a bush, a house, a boat, a barn, or a silo—and sketch it first as completely as he can. Then he draws the thing next to it, above it, below it, behind it, right and left of it, and so on as the composition grows. Relationships of size and space will be established much more readily.

Have him continue drawing, developing his values and details until he feels the composition is complete. Problems students have with defining distance can be resolved by discussing and illustrating the following principles: Objects or shapes closer are usually drawn larger; objects farther away are drawn smaller and higher up on the page; and overlapping of objects creates a subtle effect of space. Simple perspective

The most ordinary scene can become the inspiration for an expressive drawing.

rules, based on the horizon line, eye level, and vanishing points, should be suggested as techniques for the older youngster only when he indicates a need for them.

Youngsters should not be taken out on a sketching assignment without planning and preparation by the teacher. If possible, exciting destinations should be chosen beforehand. Avoid barren views or distant vistas that give little opportunity for varied space breakup. A class discussion prior to the field trip might open up several things to look for: the mood or atmosphere of the place; the unique characteristics of a building; the problems to be solved in drawing houses—the roof lines, the effect of darker values on window panes in daylight, the need to allow enough space for steps and porches; hints in making fences stand up and sidewalks lie flat; and some ways of breaking up foreground and sky. The teacher should remind the students that in drawing the landscape they may use the artists' creative prerogative of changing, adding, or simplifying what they see. The criterion is not photographic reality. If one wishes, he may add more trees or windows, change a roof line, or ignore a poster on a wall. Each decision, however, must be guided by aesthetic considerations, and the final composition should achieve unity and organization through effective grouping of forms, repetition of shapes, details and directional lines, overlapping of forms, textural interest, variety of positive and negative shapes and spaces, and a subtle balance of lights and darks.

TOP—Pencil drawing (grade 3). CENTER—Pen and ink drawing (grade 5). BOTTOM—Monoprint (grade 6).

DRAWING ANIMALS

A teacher guides the students in drawing animals.

Animal drawing, like most forms of graphic interpretation, depends a great deal on the child's thoughtful perception of the subject's significant form and
characteristics. It is commonly based on a mixture
of very careful observation, linked closely with a
sensitive and discriminatory use of line to bring out
the special and unique qualities of the animal. The
successful combination of these two requisites can
be observed in numerous master drawings of our art
heritage. Vital sketches such as Rembrandt's lion
and elephant, Eugène Delacroix's horses, or Albrecht
Dürer's rabbit and rhinoceros, all impress us with the
artist's insight into the psychological and physical
spirit of the animals.

The responsibility of developing within the child
the capacity to capture the essential form in animal
drawing rests for the most part on the teacher. He
must stimulate and encourage the youngsters through

field trips to museums, zoos, aquariums, and pet shops. Equally exciting opportunities to observe animals in action or at rest can be found at horse shows, circuses, parades, county or state fairs, or even national parks.

Pencil, pen and ink, fine felt nib markers are recommended for drawings and sketches on smaller surfaces. Charcoal, chalk, crayon, and blunt felt nib markers can be used effectively on larger papers. Surfaces to draw on may include newsprint, cream or gray manila, construction paper, bogus, brown kraft or butcher paper, shelf paper, and discarded wallpaper sample books. A simple, effective, yet inexpensive, drawing board can be made out of Upson board, a quarter inch thick, cut into rectangles 18 by 24 inches and edged with masking tape. These boards could also be used as protective surfaces on classroom desks.

A typical animal drawing project might begin with a sketching excursion to a local museum or zoo. Prior to the field trip, the teacher and children might discuss the several characteristics of the species they might encounter. The youngsters might be motivated to talk about the unique or unusual features of the various animals, their stance, action, disposition, and special physical attributes. For example, the strange textural patterns on the thick-skinned rhino, the wrinkled and rough skin of the gorilla's face, the repeated yet varied spots on the leopard, the rhythmic ring forms on the armadillo, the subtle variations of the zebra's stripes, all these and scores of other dis-

White crayon drawings on black construction paper (grade 3).

tinctive characteristics might be brought out in a class discussion.

At the sketch site, the students should be encouraged to draw large, bold forms which make the best use of the paper's proportions. The larger the animal study, the more possibility the student has to define and exploit the unique surface details or textures. These on-the-spot drawings might also include some delineation of significant details and the introduction of an expressive line to capture the spirit of the animal, rather than attempts to create a completed study. Many of the refinements in terms of composition and textural detail can be realized back in the classroom under the helpful guidance of the teacher.

For the upper-grade child selecting one animal during a field trip and developing it with a single study or series of studies is probably more beneficial than attempting to make several separate renditions in the limited time allowed away from the classroom. If scheduling permits, the teacher may plan several visits, so that the youngsters will have ample opportunity to sketch various animals. Light, tentative sketches are recommended for the first attempts, but once the basic forms are achieved, more dominant lines may be introduced to reinforce and emphasize the significant characteristics. In the initial sketches the students may wish to include detail studies of separate parts of the animals, such as the muzzle, mouth, eye, ear, tail, leg, hoof, or horn. These vignettes could be drawn in any remaining space not occupied by the main drawing.

Sketches for a dinosaur modeling project (grade 5).

Conté crayon drawing on gray manila (grade 6).

The teacher might also suggest that the students draw their animals involved in some activity or typical situation such as eating, resting, climbing, bathing, walking, running, hunting, or caring for their young. In the upper grades especially, the stance and action of each animal should be noted, because this helps the student consolidate his understanding of the form. The swinging action of a monkey, the stretching of a giraffe's neck, the sway of an elephant's trunk, or the rearing up of a horse, all serve as a means of interpreting the spirit and disposition of the animal.

Drawing the animal directly should always be encouraged, but when this prospect is out of the question, motivation through slides, film strips, or opaque projections of illustrations and photographs will provide vicarious enrichment. In the lower elementary grades the children might use the projected material for recall and clarification of forgotten details. Older students may wish to refer to the resource illustrations for a longer period, since they are quite concerned with the presentation of an accurate portrayal of the subject. Mounted photographs can often fulfill this need, but it should be definitely understood that the photo file is for reference only and not for copying or tracing.

The youngsters need to be challenged, too, to consider the importance of composition in their animal drawings. Too often an exciting animal drawing will be isolated in the middle of a page without any reference to the possibilities of negative space. To help the students in this respect, the teacher might trigger a discussion on space problems and some possible solutions, such as the introduction in the composition of other animals and plants and the utilization of characteristic habitats, such as hills, streams, sandbars, and rock formations. It should be pointed out to the students that many of these environmental aspects can be used to enhance the main subject, while at the same time creating an interesting positive-negative breakup in the drawing.

Unusual and interesting plants, fall foliage, rocks, or flowers in season might serve as inspiration for supplemental background effects. Small leaves or twigs might be drawn giant size to become jungle trees, and the pattern of the foliage could complement the textures and designs of the animals themselves. Films and slides of jungle scenery might be shown for ideas. Mounted photographs of tropical flora could be projected for further study. The possibilities of enrichment are limitless.

Both in the classroom and on supervised field trips the students should have the opportunity to draw directly from reality. Through these immediate experiences the child learns to sharpen his visual capacities and to develop his ability to express graphically his ideas and reactions. The scope of his perception is expanded through the discipline of conceiving in line those phenomena which impress and excite him. Thus the child achieves a dual compensation; he gains invaluable experience through looking, perceiving, evaluating, and depicting ,and at the same time he fulfills a real need through a personal, art expression.

TOP—*Conté crayon drawing on gray manila (grade 6).*
BOTTOM—*Felt nib pen and white tempera on gray manila (grade 6).*

LEFT—Crayon drawing on colored construction paper (grade 1). CENTER—Colored tissue over felt-nib-marker drawing (grade 3). RIGHT—Batik, wax and dye on cloth (grade 4).

THE STILL-LIFE COMPOSITION

The still life, or *nature morte* as the French artists termed this particular art arrangement, is a valid and effective approach in teaching keen observation, awareness, perception and delineation of a variety of shapes, shallow space, overlapping of forms, color, value, and renewed interest in common objects. Children from first grade on up can be encouraged to see new beauty and aesthetic form in bottles, lanterns, driftwood, fruits, vegetables, compotes, kitchen utensils and appliances. The still life is similar in many respects to a landscape, since it poses the same kind of compositional challenge.

From the third grade on up children can be guided to see the design possibilities in their still-life interpretations. The teacher should discuss the set-up of the still life and together with the youngsters arrange the objects to obtain the most aesthetic effect.

In selecting objects for a still life, utilize a variety of forms—small, short, tall, simple, complex, textured, and plain. Antique shops and secondhand stores provide a rich source of unusual and stimulating objects that contribute to exciting still-life compositions.

Collage made of assorted "found" papers (grade 4).

A classroom still-life arrangement in pen and ink (grade 6).

Eschew the trite or tasteless figurine. The place ment of the objects is important, too. Try arranging them on a desk, a table, a chair, a window ledge, or on the floor with variety of heights. Utilize over-lapping forms, and an informal balance. Use drapery or a tablecloth to suggest movement or as a unifying effect.

The more objects in a still life, providing they are arranged to allow for interesting negative areas, the more opportunity the student has for selection and rejection. In the same vein, the more objects a student utilizes in his composition the more effectively he usually builds his design.

One big question in any kind of life sketch is where does the student begin. There is no one way to begin drawing a still life. One suggestion that youngsters respond to and have success with is to have them begin by drawing an object in the center of the still life and then move to the next object that touches it and so on until they have filled their page.

Another possibility is to have the student select from the still-life material available a specific group of objects and concentrate on these as his center of interest. He then develops his sketch outward from this special area of emphasis.

Other approaches are just as valid. A light tenta-tive sketch to get the general overall composition is used by many youngsters. This preliminary drawing is then developed with values, shading, and texture into a satisfying orchestration of lines and lights and dark.

PAINTING WITH TEMPERA

Painting with tempera (opaque watercolor) is an art experience every child should have. Tempera pigments are rich, subtle, varied, tactile, and adaptable. The children can apply color over color over color to achieve special effects or easily repaint those areas that they feel do not contribute to their composition as it develops.

Though many teachers are aware of the expanding possibilities for art expression in this rich medium, large numbers of schools do not provide tempera painting activities because of the housekeeping chores involved. It is true, perhaps, that tempera projects require more preparation, more careful storage, and more expeditious cleanup procedures than watercolor or the dry cake pigments, but these factors should not rule it out of the program. During the past decade, inventive teachers and art consultants have developed

TOP—Collage of wallpaper remnants on colored construction paper (grade 4). CENTER—Crayon engraving (grade 6). BOTTOM—Crayon drawing on colored construction paper (grade 4).

71

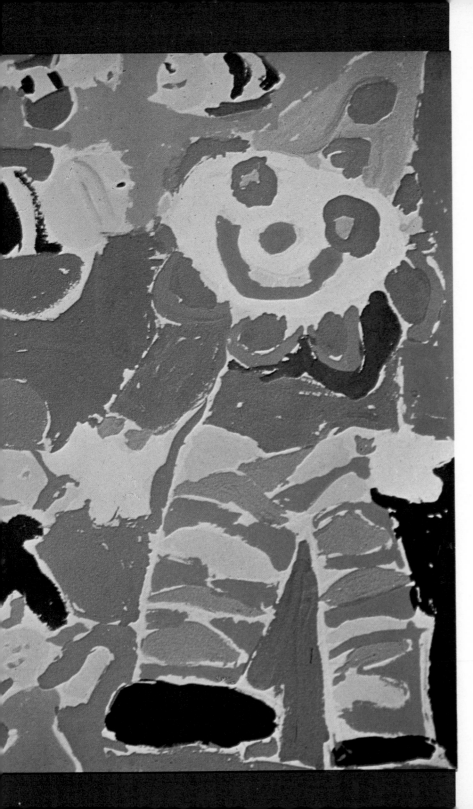

many ways to solve the problem of tempera painting where large classes and limited facilities are involved. Some of these have proven most effective and time-saving. Baby food cans, juice cans, or half-pint wax milk cartons have been successfully used as paint containers. Carrying cases for the paints have been made out of discarded cardboard cartons, pop bottle carriers, or used tumbler carry-alls. Some art instructors use economical clear plastic tumblers, covering them with clear elasticized plastic covers.

Children can help in the preparation of paint, mixing various hues, tints, and shades, and filling the individual paint containers. For a class of thirty children, about five dozen containers of paint should suffice. At least six white and six black containers should be available, the rest in a variety of hues and values. These should be placed on a table or cart that is easily accessible to all the youngsters and low enough so that the various colors are visible. There should be a clean brush for every color or container. Children take turns picking up the color they need and a brush to go with it. When they are through with a color, they return the container with the brush in it to the central supply. In this process it is advisable that the children paint using one color container at a time, although in a table situation several colors may be shared by the group.

Sufficient time should be allotted for cleanup procedures. The brushes, especially those with plastic handles and nonrusting ferrules, can be taken out of the paint containers and dropped into a dishpan of

Tempera painting on Muraltex paper (grade 1).

72

Tempera painting on Muraltex board (grade 4).

soapy water to soak over night, to be rinsed clean the next morning and stored bristle side up. The plastic covers should be put on the containers to keep the paint moist. Occasionally the dry paint should be scraped from the inner sides into the containers with a tongue depressor or blunt-edged knife, and the paint should be diluted with water if necessary. The lids or edges of the containers should be wiped off with a damp cloth, and the plastic covers rinsed out.

In the primary grades tempera painting is a natural for children. They take to it like ducks to water. First graders especially enjoy making designs in paint, and they need only the hint of stimulation to get them started. Themes such as *Explosion in a Paint Factory,*

Fourth of July Fireworks, Butterfly and Bumblebee Fight in a Flower Garden, Spring Fever, Traffic Jam, or *Planets of Outer Space* fire their imaginations and their paint brushes. Construction paper 12 by 18 inches or 18 by 24 inches in assorted colors makes an excellent background for tempera paintings, because the surface color can become part of the design. It also helps tie the composition together.

Children should be encouraged to plan their paintings whenever possible. A line drawing in white chalk rather than in pencil is usually recommended for the basic sketch. Background papers to paint on include white drawing, cream manila, gray manila, bogus, oatmeal, Muraltex board, oak tag, corrugated

Tempera painting on Muraltex board (grade 1).

board, chipboard, want-ad sections of magazines, butcher or kraft paper, and the backs of wallpaper samples or remnants. When a child begins to paint his picture, he will usually start with a color which appeals to him. While he still has this color at his desk, the teacher might suggest that he look for other places in his picture where he might repeat the color. This may help him think of using colors to achieve unity. There are some cautions, too, in tempera painting that the teacher might emphasize: "Wipe the excess paint off your brush on the lip of the container; be careful when painting next to a wet area because the two colors will run together; if you wish to paint over a color, you must wait until it is thoroughly dry; do not put your painting on top of your neighbor's picture while his is still wet."

In the upper grades the children can exploit the many exciting possibilities of tempera paint, because they are better able to control the processes. They may try designing on wet colored construction paper, dripping or spattering paint on varied papers, using the dry-brush method to achieve texture, scumbling, speckling, stippling, combining tempera with crayon, felt nib pen, collage effects, or painting on unusual surfaces or materials, such as burlap, sandpaper, papier-mâché reliefs, canvas, and windowpanes. Older children should be encouraged to mix even more tints, shades, or neutralized hues than are already available in the containers. They can use discarded pie or cake tins, muffin tins, or aluminum TV-dinner trays for this purpose. However, they should be cautioned not to mix more paint than they need. The substitute paint palettes should be rinsed out at the end of the class period.

It is important to remember that growing youngsters cannot rush through a tempera painting experience, any more than they can rush through any worthwhile effort. Sufficient time should be allotted for all phases of the project: sketching, making deliberate and sensitive color choices, developing pattern and details, and establishing a personal expression. Tempera painting, perhaps more than any other elementary art technique, expands the child's world of color and color relationships.

TEMPERA BATIK

An art project that is usually recommended for the upper grades because of its technical complexities is *tempera batik*. For the older child who has worked repeatedly in tempera throughout the grades, tempera batik, which combines tempera and black India ink, offers a stimulating variation. It demands thought and planning, plus imagination. Almost any subject idea can be interpreted in this medium, including figure composition, portrait studies, still life, and the various forms of flora and fauna. Basically the approach is similar to the standard practice of tempera painting, but some deviations from the common tempera technique are necessary. A heavier paper must be used for the painting inasmuch as it requires a wash-off or sponging process. Muraltex board and construction papers are commonly used, although heavy white drawing paper or gray manila may serve the purpose. After the sketch in white chalk is made, the painting can begin. Much of the success of this project depends on the paper surface left unpainted, because this is where the ink adheres in the final phase. If possible, open spaces should be left between object and background, where two objects meet, in patterned areas within objects, and wherever areas of black are needed for contrasting effects. For example,

TOP—*Tempera paintings on Muraltex board (grade 4).*
BOTTOM—*Tempera paintings on Muraltex board (grade 3).*

75

Tempera paint and India ink batik (grade 3).

object, lighter on the other. These chalk lines and chalk areas are then left unpainted. For the youngster who does not understand the intricacies of the empty spaces, the teacher should suggest that he paint up to the white chalk lines only, leaving them unpainted. After the tempera-painted surfaces have dried thoroughly, the whole thing is given an even coat of undiluted black India ink applied with a wide, soft-bristle brush.

One important point to remember is that it is impractical to repaint a dried tempera area because successive layers of paint are washed off in the spraying or sponging process, and only that pigment which is absorbed by the paper remains.

After a twenty-four hour drying period, the paintings can be placed on a piece of masonite, heavy plastic, or tin and washed off at the sink. To prevent overwashing certain areas, the painting should be rotated while it is rinsed. If the ink still adheres to sections where color is vital, a wet sponge can be utilized to bring it out. When the washing and rinsing process is completed, use flat paper towels to absorb excess moisture. While the paintings are still moist, they may be retouched in areas that need more color, but this should be done in a special manner with either a Q-tip or crushed paper towel to approximate the blurred quality of the technique. The dry tempera batiks can be coated with a solution of two-thirds shellac and one-third alcohol or with transparent liquid wax to enrich the colors and protect the surface.

the small interstices between fern fronds or between a bird's feathers could be left plain so that the ink would flow into these spaces and create a dark and light area. All spaces left between objects or between object and background can be varied in thickness, size, and emphasis. Exciting results in the final black pattern can be achieved by instructing the students to make their white chalk sketch in a variety of lines—heavy, delicate, thick to thin, bolder on one side of an

MURAL MAKING

If the planning and creation of a mural as a unique visual expression is to be a valid experience for the youngsters, then the requirements of mural art must be met as far as possible, or the effort made by the students will dissipate into haphazard performance. First of all, the teacher and student must decide whether the project or theme is suitable for a long-term mural undertaking. Some compositions are more appropriate and more adaptable to group projects because of their complexity and inclusiveness. For the younger children the following themes are suggested.

The Bird Aviary	The Flower Garden
Land of Make-Believe	On the Farm
The Fish Pond	Animals in the Jungle
The Supermarket	Summer Games

Older children will respond to the following ideas:

State Fair	Three-Ring Circus
Our Community	Games on the Playground
Winter Carnival	Our Expanding Universe
Homecoming Parade	The Growth of Transportation

Some pertinent questions that the teacher might ask in the presentation of a mural project are: "What is a mural? Why do artists paint murals? What do we know about the history of mural making? Who made the first murals? Are there any murals in our city, county, or state?"

"How large should our mural be? Where can we work on it? in the classroom? the hallway? the gym? the cafeteria? Where might we place the mural when we finish it? What technique or media should we use? What shall we use for our theme? How shall we decide what each one will contribute to the mural?

For example, if "Fun on the Playground" was selected as the theme and a cut-out and pin-up mural as the technique, here are some questions that might be asked: "How many different kinds of games or sports shall we portray? Make a list on the blackboard. How shall we assign these in class? by slips of paper? by rows? by tables?

"How many different areas of the playground should we identify? What pieces of playground equipment shall we portray? How shall we decide on the size of the children playing? Should we make them all the same size? What about variety? How shall the children and the teachers be dressed on the playground? What patterns are found in clothes? What kind of day will it be? What else will we want to include—trees, bushes, fences, animal pets, birds, drinking fountain, signs? How shall we compose the separate pieces? How shall we attach them to the background?"

Many media and processes can be used in making murals. Tempera paint, felt markers and watercolor, rubber brayers and water-base printing inks, oil crayon or pastel, collage (colored construction paper, cardboard, cloth remnants, yarn, etc.) or mixed techniques are all possibilities. Murals may be painted directly on the background surface or assembled after the children have completed separate parts at their desks.

In the pin-up or staple-on type of mural, as the youngsters finish their assigned pieces, they pin them up temporarily to the background cork bulletin, Celotex, wall board, or cardboard backing which may have been painted in advance. Children who finish their individual contributions first may be assigned other affinitive items to fill up the background and unify the composition. Depending on the subject matter of the mural, these might be: a sun, trees, flowers, houses, fences, stars, clouds, rock formations, insects, birds, seaweed, coral, small animals.

Sometimes students work in a small group on a large item. Mural-making offers excellent opportunities for sharing ideas.

When all the students have finished their contributions to the mural and all the separate pieces are tentatively pinned to the background, the teacher and students should devote at least one class period to arranging the mural. Here the teacher's subtle guidance is of utmost importance. He must explain that the mural is much like a giant painting and demands the same compositional factors—varied

Tempera paint and India ink batiks (grade 6).

78

sizes and heights of objects, groupings of similar objects, figures, animals, or plants for unity, interesting empty or negative areas to counterbalance the busy areas, larger objects in front and smaller ones up higher if space is to be suggested. Inevitably, there will be the problem of one child's figure partially obscuring another. Here the teacher must tact-fully smooth troubled waters by pointing out that overlapping shapes also create unity in the mural. When the separate pieces are finally rearranged into a satisfactory composition, they may be either tacked down or glued down permanently, and the mural can be displayed in the lunchroom or hallway for all the school to enjoy.

Group pin-up mural done with Sketcho (oil crayon) on Muraltex paper (grade 4).

COLLAGE

One of the most intriguing and most controversial forms of visual expression of our day has been the art of assemblage. Inheritors of Dadaism and Surrealism, the angry young men of the assemblage academy, have dug deep into the refuse and discards of our times to create pictorial constructions that revolt, intrigue, shock, titillate, and dismay the layman, as well as the art critic. A typical assemblage might consist of a dirty torn blanket spattered with paint, stained and battered tennis shoes, and a mutilated deck of cards all nailed or glued to the side of a dilapidated barn door.

Much the same kind of shock and dismay greeted the first *collage* attempts a half century ago. The innovators of the collage form, Pablo Picasso, Georges Braque, Juan Gris, and Hans Arp, bore their share

TOP—Group mural (4' x 8') made with colored construction paper on Upson board (grade 2). CENTER—Group mural drawn with Sketcho (oil crayon) on Muraltex paper (grade 4). BOTTOM—Group mural done with corrugated cardboard and assorted paper (grade 5).

A group of children paint a mural on a construction barrier (grades 1 through 6).

of sharp criticism because they detoured from the purist conventions of oil painting. Today their creations in paste, paper, and other items from the wastebasket appear relatively tame. Since the days of the Fauvists, however, the wellsprings out of which collage makers have drawn their materials have expanded so bountifully in content and variety that there are practically no limits to contemporary collage expression.

There are many approaches to the art of collage. They range from simple cutting and tearing of colored paper to complex sawing, snipping, clipping, breaking, and shearing of plywoods, plastics, cardboards, and cloth.

Some possible materials for collages are listed here for the teacher:

Colored poster and construction paper
Textured papers from magazines
Cloth remnants, rug samples
Plywoods of different veneers
Multi-colored tissue paper
Weeds, bark, leaves, seeds, sand, crushed rock
Assorted metal sheets

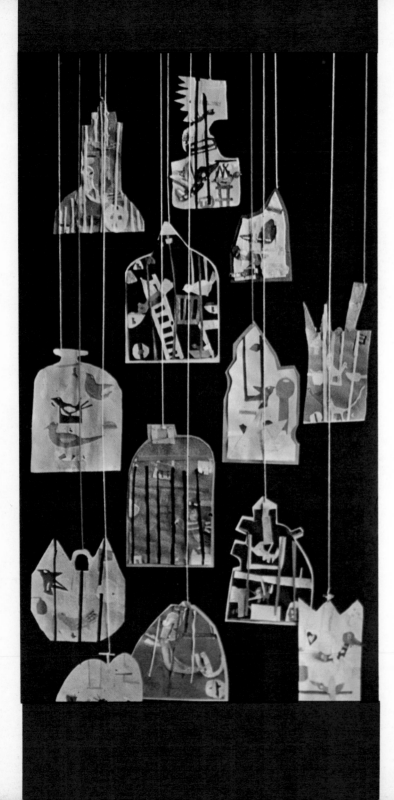

Children from the first grade up enjoy cutting and pasting, and truly, there is hardly any more adaptable medium to teach the many elements of composition: interesting shapes, overlapping to create unity and shallow depth, negative space, color relationships, balance, and rhythm.

The fact that the object or shapes the youngster cuts out can be shifted and changed about before deciding on a final arrangement gives him and the teacher a remarkable opportunity to discuss the idea he wishes to emphasize and the basic structure of his composition before he pastes or glues the separate pieces permanently. Often he finds there is more than one way to express his idea.

From the first grade on up the teacher will find many of the following suggestions useful in helping children with their collage or cut-and-paste expressions.

> Cut out your big shapes first. These will determine your general composition.
> If you are using a colored background be sure to make use of it in your overall plan. Don't cover it entirely if you wish it to help unify your composition.
> Exploit different materials for the background surface: chipboard, masonite, Upson board, plywood, corkboard, Muraltex board, vinyl, burlap stretched over board, or oak tag.
> If you are working with bold, contrasting colors, you might try repeating a color for balance or unity.
> Little shapes, details, designs, textures, or patterns can be pasted on the big shapes before the big shape is pasted down permanently.

Bird cages of colored construction paper (grade 1).

Overlapping of forms, shapes, objects, or figures can be exploited in the collage technique more successfully than in any other medium. As children grow older they begin to see the unusual shapes, the suggestion of distance, and the contrasting relationships that they can create through overlapping. This is the first major step short of actual perspective that they can take to indicate an awareness of space.

Some materials like tinfoil and shiny plastics have a strong fascination for children, and unless guided, they are apt to use them in an unrestrained, haphazard manner. Suggest their utilization as a spot of emphasis or in a neutralized fashion.

As in most pictorial designs, a quality of unity or wholeness may often be achieved through repetition of a texture, value, pattern, or shape. Here, especially, the use of informal balance may help. Instead of repeating the color or texture or pattern in exactly the same amount and in direct balance, the amount, weight, size, or shape of each repeated factor might be varied to create subordinate emphases.

There is an old Chinese admonition that might help the youngsters compositionally. It deals with the aesthetic beauty of the *uneven number of things or motifs in an arrangement*. Three and five rather than two or four. The same principle could be utilized in the repetition of color, value, texture, or pattern areas.

Use the pages of discarded magazines as paste-applying surfaces. When the student needs a clean pasting area, he just turns another page.

(See Appendix E for a listing of materials useful in the making of a collage)

Collage of colored construction paper (grade 1).

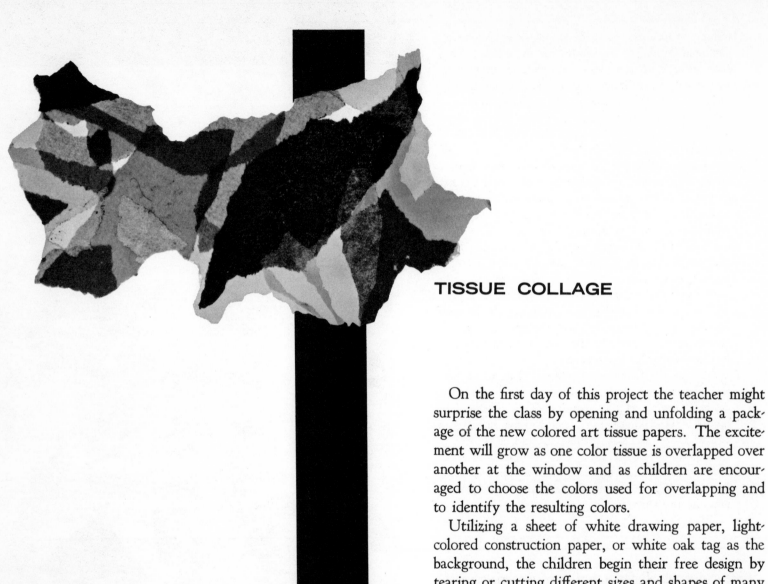

TISSUE COLLAGE

On the first day of this project the teacher might surprise the class by opening and unfolding a package of the new colored art tissue papers. The excitement will grow as one color tissue is overlapped over another at the window and as children are encouraged to choose the colors used for overlapping and to identify the resulting colors.

Utilizing a sheet of white drawing paper, light-colored construction paper, or white oak tag as the background, the children begin their free design by tearing or cutting different sizes and shapes of many colors of tissue, giving them a sparse coat of rubber cement, white liquid glue, or shellac diluted some‐ what with methanol or alcohol, and pasting them down, overlapping the shapes as they go along. It is advisable that they begin with the lighter tissue colors first in order to create new colors through overlapping.

One idea that will help to avoid a lot of "sticky" problems is to use discarded magazines, in lieu of newspapers, as pasting surfaces and suggest that yonngsters turn to a different page of the magazine each time they apply paste to a shape. With this process they have a clean pasting area each time without using up too much work space.

As the children's compositions build up they should be encouraged to look for hints of faces, animals, birds, figures, or trees. Deeper colors of tissue can be introduced to create darker areas and enrich the value potential. Once a partial figure or animal is discovered, it can be given more significance by adding pieces of tissue to indicate arms, legs, horns, beaks, hats, tails, or other appendages that characterize its form. To strengthen the allover com‐ position the background may be subdued by pasting pieces of gray or complementary colored tissues over it, thus emphasizing the figure. Crayon, ink, felt nib pen, or tempera paint in black, white, and gray can be used to add exciting linear texture to a figure or form—bark lines on a tree, hair lines on a head, fur lines on an animal, or feather lines on a bird. Details, textures, and patterns can be utilized to enhance or enrich the background to give contrast to the figure.

TOP—Materials organization for tissue collage. CENTER, BOTTOM—Colored tissue collages combined with felt nib pen drawings (grades 3 and 4).

MOSAICS

The multi-faceted and colorfully sparkling technique of mosaic has found its way into the elementary art program to enrich the art experiences of the youngsters. It is a welcome but challenging addition to the repertoire of child expression. It involves special materials, often special tools, a longer studio schedule, adequate, organized storage, and a teacher with infinite patience. Primary children work with simple materials such as construction paper and magazine advertisements, while the upper-grade pupils can use vinyl or ceramic tile.

Motivation for the project might be visits to see contemporary mosaic murals in churches, civic centers, hospitals, hotels, schools, and business establishments. Compositional ideas for mosaics that are adaptable to the elementary art program, yet simple and exciting enough to interest young chil-

dren, might include: *Birds among Foliage, Birds in a Cage, Fish in the Sea, Fish in an Aquarium, Animals in Their Habitats, Insects and Leaves, Flowers in a Garden, The Circus, and The Fair.*

In mosaic design, as in almost all two-dimensional projects, an important basic step is the preliminary sketch from life, from museum visits, or from reference films, slides, and photographs. These sketches are then developed into a satisfactory composition and drawn on paper, the same size as the final mosaic. Usually one object is emphasized, but considerations of secondary emphases through repetition of the motif on a smaller scale can be made. The children should be encouraged to see and interpret the characteristic features, such as beaks on birds, horns on animals, or eyes and gills on fish. An effective light and dark contrasting design that can be later translated in terms of the colored tesserae should be developed.

This sketch is then transferred directly or by carbon paper to the final background material. Colored construction paper, mounting board, chipboard, oak tag, masonite, or plywood can be used for this surface depending on the process.

One of the biggest factors in the success of mosaic projects is the effective organization of materials and tools. There must be an adequate supply of tesserae material whether it be paper, vinyl, or clay. In the case of construction paper, strips of paper can be precut and organized according to color in shoe boxes or tote trays. Similar storage facilities could be provided for vinyl scraps. The nature of the many types

Collages made with "found objects" on masonite or cardboard (grade 6).

87

Scrap vinyl mosaic on masonite surface; process recommended for upper grades only (grade 5).

of vinyl or plastic material varies, and only special types can be cut with tinsnips. Others will have to be broken with a hammer. Students should wear welder's goggles or rubber swim masks as a precautionary measure when breaking hard vinyl.

Suggested adhesives for paper mosaic include thinned-down school paste, rubber cement, or a diluted white glue. Adhesives for vinyl or glass mosaics include full-strength white glues or plastic and tile cements.

Students take turns at the general supply boxes, selecting the color tesserae they wish to use first. They may concentrate on a significant feature of an important object or motif—the eye of a bird, the design in a butterfly wing, the petal of a flower—and begin the gluing process. They should be guided to employ directional movements in applying the tesserae and to avoid a brick-laying, precise technique. Open spaces between tesserae are very important.

There should be consistency in the tessera placement but not monotonous perfection of spacing. Tesserae should not be cut in exactly the same size. They can be squares, off-squares, rectangles, triangles, or uneven and faceted shapes. Rounded, amorphous tesserae should be avoided, if possible, since these tend to negate the mosaic quality.

Emphasize form through the contrasting colors of a wing against a body, a petal against the center of a flower, or an eye against a head. An important consideration is the employment of several values of a color in large areas, like the body of an animal or in the background—many values of blues, instead of only one, for a sky or sea treatment; many values of greens for foliage interpretation; or many browns, ochres, and umbers for the earth.

The brightest or darkest colors can be exploited for rich emphasis, in the beak or claw of a bird, the iris of an eye, the stripes of a zebra fish, the antennae of a moth, or the plumage of a bird.

A workable homemade grout can be made utilizing a dry mix of half powdered silica sand and half plaster of Paris, or a mix of half marble dust and half plaster of Paris. A pure plaster of Paris mixture can be used if other additions are unavailable. Add the mix to water in a rubber or plastic container until islands of mix appear on the surface of the water. Stir by hand to remove lumps, but do not over stir. When the mixture reaches a thick, creamy consistency, pour it on the center of the tesserated surface, and, using your hand, spread the mixture evenly between the tesserae. A sponge, rag, or paper towel may be used to remove excess grout from the tesserated surfaces, but pressure should not be so heavy that grout is dislocated from between the tesserae. A film of plaster will still remain on the tesserae, but this can be removed once the grouting is dry by scrubbing with a rag or soft brush. Grouted surfaces may be stained with oil or water-base colors to unify and enhance the mosaic composition. A commercial floor wax can be applied to the completed vinyl mosaic to heighten the color and protect the grouted surfaces.

VEGETABLE PRINTS

Printmaking in the elementary art program is another area of design that holds much excitement for the children, but print techniques should be carefully programmed by the teacher, so that they range from simple processes in the lower grades to complex material and tool exploitation at the upper level.

Some of the most exciting and colorful allover designs can be made by very young children using common materials such as vegetables, bars of soap, clay stamps, and "found" objects like buttons, spools, flat clothespins, or corks. Caution must be taken with cutting tools. Sloyd knives, nails, blunt scissors, melon scoopers, and serrated plastic picnic knives can be used by the primary grades for creating designs in vegetables.

Students should be encouraged to work for a bold, simplified breaking up of space. Possible design motifs on the vegetables might include wedgecuts,

Construction paper mosaics. TOP, BOTTOM—Grade 3. CENTER—Grade 5.

crosscuts, circular cuts, and assorted holes, always with the negative and positive design factor in mind. Vegetables must be fresh and crisp for controlled carving. A number of methods may be utilized to ink the vegetables stamps: direct brush application with tempera or watercolors, a saturated ink pad using tempera or monoprint medium, or water-base printing inks on a masonite square or a cookie tin. Children should have a wide choice of printing papers to choose from: colored construction, colored tissue, gray manila, bogus, oatmeal, or newspaper. The children should be reminded of the design and pattern possibilities in this project, instead of allowing them to merely manipulate the materials in a random fashion. Preliminary experimentation by the child with the blocks on scrap paper could provide the necessary understanding of the process.

The teacher should encourage the child to plan his composition row by row, so that a different yet organized pattern emerges. The imperfection of the child's attempt at a controlled pattern often lends a naïve quality to the product. The youngsters will find that by sharing their vegetable blocks they can produce unusual variations on a theme. Although the conventional method of the vegetable stamp per se has its merits, the embellishment of the completed vegetable prints with a number of additional media can add excitement, charm, sparkle, and variety. One of the most successful ways to augment a vegetable or clay stamp print is by the application of crayon, Craypas, Sketcho, or chalk to the negative spaces

Potato print done with tempera paint and colored chalk on colored construction paper (grade 2).

between the individual printed areas. Again students could be guided to create unity in their allover design by allowing some of the paper to show between printed areas. For older students even more complex supplementation can be suggested or introduced. The use of India ink either in a linear rendering or by the *tempera batik* method, experimentation with wax resist and encaustics, collage appliqué, and colored-tissue overlay, all can enhance the basic print pattern.

Students will find many uses for their completed works including book jackets, box covers, place mats, shelf paper, room divider decorations, lamp shades, or scrapbook covers.

TOP LEFT—Cutting the linoleum surface for a print (grade 3). ABOVE—Planning the tissue background for the linoleum print (grade 4). BOTTOM LEFT—The linoleum print on the colored tissue background (grade 3).

CARDBOARD PRINTS

Printmaking in its many forms is a worthwhile and recommendable activity for children at all levels. The problem often facing the teacher is just what medium or technique should be utilized at each stage of the child's growth. Potato, "found" object, or clay stamp prints are feasible for primary grades one and two. However, when youngsters reach the third and fourth grade they become interested in and challenged by more complex, more sophisticated approaches in printmaking. Cardboard printmaking with its varied yet controlled possibilities offers this kind of excitement and exploitation. Results are often similar to wood or linoleum block prints and the adaptability of rearranging the design before gluing is an important and significant feature.

Potato prints (grade 2).

Materials for this project may be few and simple or limitless and complex depending on the ability and readiness of the children. For the youngsters with little previous experience, the following materials and tools are recommended: a piece of heavy cardboard cut to the size of the desired print, oak tag or thin cardboard (chipboard) similar to the kind laundries use in shirt packaging, glue or mucilage, scissors, ink brayer or roller, water-base printing inks, shellac, brush, alcohol or methanol to clean out the shellac brush, paper punch, and pinking shears.

Subject matter for cardboard prints is limitless. It can be anything the child sees or imagines. However, there should be the same emphasis on design and composition as in any other project. Especially important is the utilization of a variety of shapes that fill the space of the cardboard piece the child has chosen. A practical background size for this age group consists of 9- by 9-inch, 12- by 12-inch, or 9- by 12-inch rectangles and squares or circles or ovals of a similar size. Pieces much larger than this create a problem in a big class, especially during the printing process. Storage of work in progress is important, and the use of large envelopes or folders with the children's names on them is suggested.

TOP—Drawing and cutting cardboard prints (grade 3). CENTER—Gluing the separate pieces on the cardboard background for the print. BOTTOM—Inking the cardboard plate.

When the children have cut their separate positive shapes out of the oak tag or chipboard and have created negative patterns in these shapes using a paper punch, scissors, a single-edge razor blade, or an X-acto knife, they arrange these on the background cardboard until a satisfactory composition is obtained. They may see a need for more shapes to fill the space, or they may want to shift the center of interest. When the youngster, with the teacher's guidance, achieves a workable design, he glues the separate pieces to the cardboard. It is important that all edges are glued down securely. The whole composition is then given a coat of shellac to seal it and to prevent the separate pieces from dissolving and coming apart during the printing or cleaning process.

The inking and printing phase of this project is, of course, the most exciting aspect for the youngsters, but unless the teacher has planned this activity carefully, it can develop into a chaotic misadventure.

The teacher must be certain that she has an adequate supply of inking squares, (one-quarter-inch thick masonite pieces, one foot square, shellacked or lacquered, are recommended) rubber brayers or rollers, water-base printing inks and printing papers (newsprint takes a very fine impression) including

A cardboard print (grade 3).

poster paper in assorted colors, cream or gray manila, tissue paper in white and colors, and colored sections from magazines.

In a typical classroom situation, averaging between 25 and 35 students, it might be wise to let four to six youngsters ink and print at one time at a table provided for them in a section of the room where a sink is handy. Let them first attempt a one-color ink impression, perhaps black. Then if they wish they might try a multi-color print. Care must be taken when washing the cardboard plate. Sometimes it is wiser to let the ink dry on the plate overnight. The process of taking a print should be demonstrated for the whole class so that it does not have to be repeated for each group making a print. All prints should be put in slots, on shelves, or spring-clipped to a clothes-line to dry overnight.

Cardboard prints (grade 3).

Finished prints can be mounted attractively for display purposes. Children should be encouraged to exchange prints with one another. The cardboard plate itself can be inked, mounted, and displayed.

Children in the upper grades can exploit the cardboard print technique even further through the use of additional materials to create textural effects including corrugated paper, heavy string or cord, burlaps, textured wallpaper, masking tape, and a variety of "found" textures.

TOP—Cardboard-print mural (grade 3). BOTTOM—Pulling the cardboard print.

Felt-pen sketch for a linoleum print (grade 4).

LINOLEUM PRINTS

An exciting and complex form of printmaking recommended for the upper elementary art classes is linoleum block printing. The unmounted battleship gray linoleum suggested for this project may be obtained from school supply houses or from furniture stores. Basic tools needed are linoleum cutting gouges #1, #2, #3, #4, and #5, plus a handle, rubber brayer (ink roller), inking slab, and printing press (optional).

Preliminary drawings or sketches in pencil, black crayon, pen and ink, or felt marker are important requisites for a successful printmaking unit because they determine the basic composition, including the center of interest, the dark and light pattern, and the textural possibilities. The teacher and young student must be aware that the linoleum gouge makes its own unique lines and indentures, and although it does not lend itself to the same control as a pencil or brush, it often produces effects that are more direct, honest, and naïve. All the various gouges should be exploited to their fullest extent for both linear and solid effects.

Subject matter for linoleum prints is unlimited, but students will usually find many possibilities for composition and textural exposition in birds, insects, mammals, fish, reptiles, old houses, portraits, mythological heroes, Biblical and legendary figures, and still life including musical instruments, antiques, household objects, plant forms, or combinations of any of these.

After a compositional sketch has been made, the student may draw it on the linoleum surface with the suggested sketching media or transfer it to the linoleum with carbon. There are various methods for initial gouging of the block. One way is to cut an outline of the composition using a veiner #1 or #2. Another process is to work from the inside out on all areas to be removed, thus minimizing an outlined emphasis.

In large classes and where materials are limited, proofs of the blocks in process can be taken in an economical yet effective manner by placing a sheet of newsprint or tissue paper over the linoleum block

Linoleum print made from a museum sketch (grade 5).

Linoleum prints (grade 5).

and using the side of a black crayon, Craypas, or Sketcho, rubbing over it carefully and with pressure. A definitive proof print will develop which will give the student a clue to his progress.

Either water-base or oil ink may be used for the final prints, although water-base inks are recommended in situations where expeditious cleanup procedures are a vital factor. The ink may be rolled out on a cookie tin, glass sheet, or masonite slab using a rubber brayer. When it feels "tacky," it is applied to the linoleum block. There are several ways to take the print. The child may put the paper on the inked block and apply even pressure with a rubber brayer, a spoon, or the palm of the hand. Another method is to place a heavy pad of newspapers on the floor, put the block face down on the paper to be printed, and step on the block using all one's weight. Commercial block printing presses may also serve the purpose.

A variety of papers may be used for block printing purposes including newsprint, brown kraft or butcher paper, colored tissue, tableau paper, construction paper, and gray or cream manila.

One effective way to display linoleum prints is by the Japanese scroll technique. Print the block on newsprint paper, leaving an inch border. Cut brown kraft paper in scroll shape and attach stained dowel rods at each end by overlaying the paper around them and gluing tightly with rubber cement. Use rubber cement to adhere the print to the scroll, allowing for effective margins.

TOP—Linoleum print (grade 5). BOTTOM—Linoleum print (grade 6).

CRAYON

The wax crayon has been a standard art medium in the elementary school for a half century or more. During the past two decades resourceful teachers have combined it with other media to provide excitement and variety for art programs. These new mixed techniques, including crayon engraving, crayon resist, and multi-crayon engraving, are described elsewhere in this chapter.

However, the many and unusual possibilities of crayon per se with its own singular merits have not always been fully exploited and evaluated. The common classroom expressions in crayon are usually weak in color intensity, in value contrasts, and in textural quality. Crayon is used too often as a pallid

TOP—*Crayon sketch on white drawing paper (grade 4).*
CENTER—*Melted crayon painting on sandpaper (grade 6).*
BOTTOM—My Family, *crayon on colored construction paper (grade 2).*

102

sketchy coloring pencil, instead of the rich, glowing, waxy, vital medium it can be. It is important that potential crayon techniques be taught from the first grade on, if the youngster is to grow in crayon expression.

A period of manipulation, exploration, and experimentation with the various colors is recommended. The teacher may prompt the children to press harder with the crayon in order to achieve richer colors; point out juxtaposition of contrasting colors; emphasize multi-colored designs—stripes, plaids, dots, circles, random curves, or cross hatching; and stress utilization of unusual colors, such as silver, gold, copper, or subtle tints, plus black, gray, and white. Older children should be encouraged to see that all applications of the crayon can be characteristic, directional, and meaningful.

The whole mood of a crayon composition changes when color is applied on different surfaces. Suggest that the children try colored construction paper as a background for their crayoning. Youngster and teacher alike will be surprised and elated by the subtleties of crayon on black, brown, blue-green, purple, or red-orange papers. Children can learn to see how their compositions tie together more effectively when they let some of the background surface show. When colored paper is used for a project, have the children try out the colors on the back of the paper to discover how the paper neutralizes the chromatic intensity of each crayon.

Preliminary sketches for crayon projects should be done with a light crayon, white, pink, or some other tint, rather than with pencil. Completed crayon compositions may be given a glowing sheen by rubbing over them with a folded towel.

The most recurring problem the teacher faces is the child who rushes through his crayon drawing, who colors in one or two sketchy objects and says he is finished, or who limits himself to two or three "coloring book" hues. There are no easy remedies for any of these occurrences, but one of the best procedures for success in crayoning projects is well-planned motivations that lead to a developed and thought-out preliminary drawing of the child's ideas as a springboard for the final crayon application.

CRAYON ENGRAVING

Crayon engraving has become a standard project in the elementary school, but its many and varied possibilities have not been fully explored. Students are too often contented with just a few hasty, random scribbled lines or patterns. The wide range of textural discoveries has been neglected, and the combination of crayon engraving with other media to augment and enhance it still needs investigation. Basically the crayon engraving technique is a linear process, and, therefore, subject matter or design which emphasizes line, texture, and pattern is best suited to this medium: animals like the porcupine,

Crayon engravings (grade 4).

anteater, and armadillo; fish of all kinds; birds, especially those of exotic plummage; reptiles such as turtles, iguanas, and horned toads; insects such as dragonflies, bees, praying mantes, and beetles; crustaceans such as crabs and crayfish; all varieties of plant life; and exciting buildings with textural effects.

Background surfaces can be white drawing paper and white or manila oak tag. The application of the crayons can take several forms, but in each it must be applied evenly and heavily so that no part of the paper shows. Newspaper padding under the paper while crayoning will help produce an even, rich coating of crayon.

The student may use a scribble design with a light crayon to determine his color areas; he may apply swatches of color that overlap; or he can correlate his colors in a free manner to coincide with the final engraving. A limited or full color range can be utilized for the crayon background depending upon the mood or feeling or atmosphere to be achieved. The next decision concerns the color of tempera to apply over the crayoned background. In most instances this has been limited to black, but there are new possibilities to be achieved by using gray, brown, or even white tempera. This multiple choice, however, introduces a problem because the student must correlate his crayon color scheme with his paint overlay; for example, if he wishes to use white as a coating, he will probably have to use deeper and darker crayons in his composition; if he uses black, it might be well for him to avoid crayoning with black or brown. The tempera should be of a thin, creamy consistency, and in order to adhere to the crayon surface, it must be conditioned with a small amount of liquid soap, approximately a tablespoonful to a pint of tempera. Too much soap in the tempera will give it a cloudy cast when dry.

The student transfers his sketch or drawing to the painted surface using either white dressmaker's carbon or regulation carbon paper depending on the color of the painted surface. A preliminary outline engraving is usually made using either a nail, compass point, or a scratch pen. Next the textural areas are delineated using a variety of linear tools including pointed dowel sticks, old dental tools, corrugated nails, sloyd knives, or pincushion plant frogs. Sharp contrasts can be achieved by scraping some areas down to the surface of the crayon. These are especially effective when they form part of the negative design space.

After the engraving process is completed, some subtle effects can be achieved by superimposing a soft crayon, Sketcho, or Craypas texture, over either the solid painted surfaces or over the engraved areas.

MULTI-CRAYON ENGRAVING

A crayon engraving process that offers limitless possibilities and a special opportunity for unusual color effects and glazes is *multi-crayon-over-crayon engraving*.

This is basically an intaglio process depending on incised line as the dominant discipline and can be a part of the student's creative repertoire from grade one on. For this process, wax crayons and a paper surface with a strong, smooth finish are required. Suggested papers are white, cream, or colored oak tag, index (bristol board), or the hard-surfaced cardboards that come with laundered shirts.

Multi-crayon engraving (grade 4).

All crayon colors can be utilized, but it is sometimes advantageous to use a limited color scheme. It is also frequently advisable to begin with a smooth, solid first layer of light crayon—yellow, pink, orange, or light blue. Successive layers can be applied over this, working from light to dark and back to light as preferred. For each progressive layer the crayon should be applied on its side in a swift definite pressure with each coating in a different stroking direction. Too much crayon pressure can be detrimental since it tends to pick up previous layers. One can apply different color sequences in different areas or cover the entire surface with one color at a time.

A tissue or a paper towel may be rubbed over the entire surface before beginning the engraving process. Transferring the preliminary sketch to the crayoned surface can be achieved by simply pressing with the point of a pencil at several strategic places in the drawing during transfer process. However, it is recommended that students engrave directly on the finished surface using their sketches or line drawings as a reference point. This brings a spontaneity and an immediacy to the work.

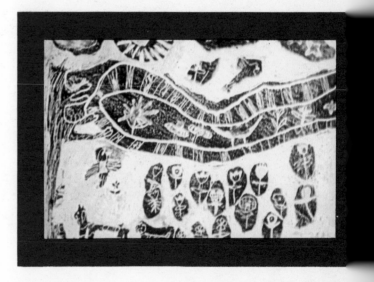

Tools which are most effective for the engraving effects are: Nails, forks, pointed dowel sticks, compass points, sloyd knives, and popsicle sticks. The sloyd knife with its blunt edge produces either a bold line or a subtle surface and does not cut or tear the paper. Discarded butter knives will also work effectively.

Multi-crayon engravings (grade 1).

For children in the primary grades, a 9- by 12-inch piece of oak tag is recommended for this project. The crayon rubbing is time consuming, and their working span is limited. However, they tackle the technique with enthusiasm and verve, and the color combinations they come up with are unusual and evocative. Here again the teacher should not limit them on the variety of color they may use. It may range from yellow to blue to gold to melon to purple to white. There should be a clear demonstration, however, of the application of the crayon in which teacher and students are both involved.

In the intermediate grades, larger sheets of oak tag or other suggested papers may be used. Students may experiment on a small piece of paper first to see the effects of color-on-color. When a multi-crayon picture is engraved first in line, then in textures, and finally developed into a light and dark pattern, it may be stained or glazed using an acrylic polymer medium which comes in a range of subtle colors: sepia, raw and burnt umber, raw and burnt sienna, chrome-oxide green. With a soft cloth and water as a diluent, the paint is rubbed over the surface and then wiped off. The thicker the paint is applied and the longer it remains on the surface, the darker the stain will be. Stains are especially effective on surfaces where the primary colors of the crayon are raw and loud.

Multi-crayon engraving brings an added aesthetic dimension to the use of the common crayon. It opens up a whole new world of color for the elementary school youngster. Try it!

Multi-crayon engravings (grade 5).

CRAYON RESIST

The insect world provides a wealth of inspiration for children's drawings, prints, and paintings, and especially for wax crayon resist techniques. Youngsters are excited by the variety of insects found in their environment, and the teacher can further stimulate participation by having the students collect specimens and bring them to class. Other sources such as illustrated texts on insects, films, and color slides will help broaden the child's awareness of insect life and give him a richer understanding of its limitless variety.

There is, however, a more aesthetic reason for introducing insects as subject matter in the elementary art program, because in the structure of almost every insect, one finds various aspects and components of design: the filigree pattern of a butterfly's wings, the contrasting motifs on a cicada's back, the rhythmic or repeated segments of a grasshopper's abdomen, the simplicity of symmetrical balance in a ladybug, and the curvilinear grade of a spider's legs.

Crayon-watercolor resist paintings (grades 2 and 3).

In a crayon-resist interpretation the pattern design of the insects is most important. The different kinds and sizes of insects guarantee variety in the composition. Usually the more insects a child uses in his composition, the richer and more complex the design becomes, and even the negative spaces evolve into exciting and unusual shapes. The environmental as-

pects lead to the overall unity. Background flowers, weeds, grasses, trees, branches, rock formations, webs, vines, and multiple floral forms all help tie the composition together.

A successful crayon-resist composition depends upon certain technical procedures that the children must understand clearly. The crayoning must be

Crayon-watercolor resist (grade 2).

done on white drawing or construction paper with a heavy pressure so that the rich quality of the wax medium is evident. A good way to insure this proper application is to use several newspapers as padding under the crayoning. In order to capitalize on the full effect of this process the student must plan to leave certain background areas uncrayoned, as well as sections within the insects and plants. Unusual colors of crayon may also be exploited: white, silver, gold, copper, gray, and other intermediate neutral hues.

When all the objects are crayoned, two processes of resist procedures can be used. They are the dry or wet methods. In the dry technique the student merely paints with watercolors, water-diluted tempera, or colored inks lightly over his crayon drawing. If the crayon has not been applied heavily enough, tempera paint will obliterate the crayon composition, but this situation can sometimes be corrected by running water over the paper to remove the excess tempera.

In the wet process the desks should be covered with newspapers. Then the student thoroughly soaks his crayon drawing in a pan or pail of water or at the sink and brings it to his desk. He then drops or floats the watercolor or diluted tempera on a selected area. One successful way of doing this is to load the brush with a color and to touch the edges of the crayoned objects letting the color flow freely. Sometimes white unpainted areas can be quite effective. For a large class a teacher might prepare before hand containers of diluted tempera or watercolor in neutral colors, and a special table could be set aside at the back of the room for the water resist process.

An exciting crayon resist can be achieved by using deep-colored construction paper as a background, instead of the usual white, cream, or gray manila. Let the youngsters try unusual crayon colors like white, silver, or gold on these colored backgrounds and then apply a wash of watercolor or diluted tempera.

A unique effect takes place, too, when the student applies crayon on green, orange, brown, blue, turquoise, red, or lavender construction paper and then coats the crayon drawing with black or white tempera. After allowing the paint to dry for a few minutes, the students wash off a film of the tempera at the sink using a sheet of masonite, tin, or heavy plastic under the drawing, so that the drawing will not tear in the process of washing. The tempera will adhere to the edges of the crayon objects to create a batik effect. In using watercolor washes for resist projects, the teacher must remember that the color always looks two or three times as potent when it is wet as when it dries, and, therefore, students must be encouraged to use stronger pigments for richer effects. In some cases the finished crayon resists may be shellacked to bring out a richer value in the paint.

The technique of crayon resist can be used just as effectively for other subject matter, including birds, fish, flowers, the circus, abstract designs, and imaginative themes.

CLAY

Every youngster in the elementary school should have the opportunity to create in clay. Clay is flexible, plastic, pliable, adaptable, and impressionable, but at the same time unpredictable, unstable, resisting, and messy. It is true that some children will respond to it more enthusiastically than others, but all youngsters can benefit from the experiences provided by this basic three-dimensional medium.

The very young child in grades one and two is a natural clay manipulator. He pats, presses, pokes, pounds, squeezes, rolls, and pinches the moist clay. He explores all its possibilities.

No two youngsters will tackle clay modeling in the same manner. Some may pull out shapes from the basic form; some may add pieces and build. Some may begin a figure with the main body; others may start with the appendages. The teacher's responsibility at this early stage is to provide an adequate supply of workable clay (a ball the size of a grapefruit for each child should suffice), some protection for desks or tables, and just enough stimulating motivation to get the child started.

The animal kingdom provides a wealth of inspiration for the young clay artist. Four-legged mammals, such as cows, horses, elephants, hippos, bears, and rhinos, are especially recommended because the child can make them stand up with ease. Human figures are a little more difficult to model, unless the child is guided to construct thick, sturdy legs that will hold the figure in balance. Trees with strong trunks are often depicted.

The primary child is especially interested in the mobility and malleability of clay. He may tell a whole story with one figure such as a clown, manipulating it to create various postures. His clown may stand on his head, bend backwards, and move his arms to portray several actions. Clay for the young child fulfills a definite kinesthetic function and need.

Some technical assistance may have to be given the young child who is having difficulty with his clay construction. The teacher might suggest a simple way to make the appendages, such as arms and legs, adhere strongly to the main body. For youngsters who can understand, the process of scoring and welding might be explained. Supports of supplementary clay pieces to counteract sagging may be introduced. At all times the teacher should point out the importance of a sturdy, simple, yet characteristic, interpretation.

Though many children at this stage are not concerned with details, there will always be those who find excitement in experimenting with textures on their clay sculptures. A collection of "found" objects: popsicle sticks, bottle caps, nails, plastic forks, buttons, shells and beads will rekindle their interest in

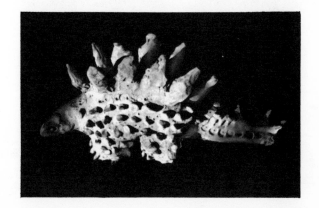

TOP—The young child stretches his imagination in clay (grade 1). CENTER—Fired clay reliefs (upper grades). BOTTOM—Dinosaurs made of fired terra cotta challenge the skill of the older child (grade 5).

Clay pots, stained and waxed over bisque (grade 3).

the process. All "found" objects should be washed or cleaned before use.

When youngsters reach the third and fourth grade level, they are much more successful with the challenging complexities of clay modeling. They are beginning to understand more clearly its inherent limitations and its rich possibilities. They ask for specific help with the technical problems of proportion, balance, and delineation of features.

At this intermediate stage a number of effective motivations should be incorporated in the teacher's repertoire. Sketching animals at the zoo, farm, fair, or museum; slides from a natural history museum; characteristic photographs of animals; films and filmstrips; pets brought to class; and reproductions of animal drawings, paintings, or sculpture by renowned artists; all will help augment the youngster's expressive potential. If the current project happens to be clay pots, a visit to a college ceramic department or a contemporary potter's studio will provide unique stimulation and authoritative answers to a number of questions.

As a subject for clay sculpture, the prehistoric dinosaur fires the imagination of the older child. The youngster is developing a strong interest in science, in the wonders of the universe; the theme of earth's first creatures intrigues him. Perhaps he has learned that skeletons of prehistoric animals have been found in the United States. He may even have seen the monstrous skeletons in a museum of natural history. Or perchance he has avidly read some of the fascinatingly illustrated books on dinosaurs. The dinosaur, indeed, lends itself quite well to interpretation in clay—the characteristic mass of the creature—ponderous, lumbering, monumental, the reptile's claylike color, the rough and wrinkled skin—all evoke the quality of earth itself.

A short period of exploration with the clay should precede every ceramic project, especially in the upper grades. The youngsters need to get the feel of the clay before tackling their idea. During this orientation process, the teacher might discuss with the class the proper plasticity of the clay, keeping excess clay moist by rolling crumbs into the main lump; some mechanics of scoring and welding clay, including the strengthening of joints by the addition of clay, the use of slip, supplemental supports for sagging parts, and finally the sharing of various cleanup and storage responsibilities.

A preliminary drawing for clay modeling projects in the upper grades is optional, though quite often it clarifies in the student's mind the type of dinosaur or other animal he plans to execute and helps him identify textural possibilities. Sometimes his dinosaur may be a creature combining the characteristics of a number of prehistoric monsters.

On a dinosaur project the teacher may have to allot a greater amount of clay to each student than suggested earlier for primary grade activities. In any case, extra prepared clay should always be ready for emergencies.

DINOSAUR BATTLE, *modeled in clay, was done as a group project (grade 5).*

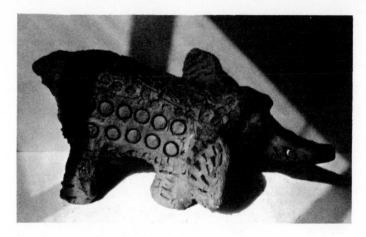

Designs created with "found objects" in clay (grade 2).

For students who need help in beginning their dinosaur, a fundamental body form based on the *post and lintel* structure may be suggested. A lump of clay slightly larger than a grapefruit is rolled out into a thick, heavy coil to form the body, tail, and neck of the animal. For the legs, sturdy, massive columns are formed and attached securely to the body and fused at the joint with additional clay. No armature or interior supports, such as wire, swab sticks, or twigs, should be used in order to prevent uneven shinkage and cracking. This is especially important if the clay is to be fired.

More discussion by teacher and student should bring out the structural possibilities that give character to the specific dinosaur: sway of body, stance or counterstance of leg, swing of tail, turn of head, action of jaws, or flare of wings.

At all stages of modeling, the animal should be turned around on its base (a piece of masonite, vinyl floor tile, or heavy cardboard, approximately twelve inches square will do), so the youngster can develop the form as three-dimensionally as possible.

There are no limits to the textural exploitations the older children can indulge in. Whether it is a clay pot, a bas-relief, a figure, or animal, the field is wide open. The "found" object collection will again provide a welcome source for texture-making tools. To achieve the peculiar scaly and armorlike skin of some dinosaurs, students have sometimes rolled out small balls or ribbons of clay and applied them to the main body of the animal with slip. Others may try combs, broken band-saw blades, forks, pencils, bottle caps, bark, screening, bolt heads, or a combination of these to create unique textural surfaces.

Where firing of the clay animals is not possible, the clay may be conditioned by adding powdered dextrin to the mixture. This process makes the clay quite hard when it dries.

If a kiln is available and the dinosaurs are to be fired, they should be allowed to dry evenly until leather hard. In the case of massive animals, small holes should be drilled or carved in their understructure and other sections of the body where they won't show when the animal is displayed. These apertures allow the moisture to escape and prevent cracking or exploding during the firing.

Stains or patinas are optional for fired clay projects in the intermediate grades. Some glaze possibilities are: walnut shoe or furniture polish, turpentine-diluted oil paints in neutral, subdued earth pigments, dirt or mud rubbed over a preliminary oil stain, or white glue over oil stain. Clear wax in paste or liquid form may be applied to protect the patina and add a soft sheen.

At the fifth and sixth grade levels, even more sophisticated clay projects can be programmed. Pots combining both coil and slab procedures provide functional as well as aesthetic challenges. Bas-reliefs, clay mosaics, and complex figure or animal compositions will keep the growing youngster interested in art at this critical period in his development.

Plaster reliefs from clay negative impressions (grades 3 and 4).

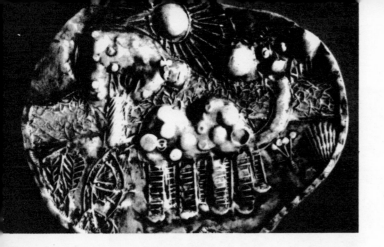

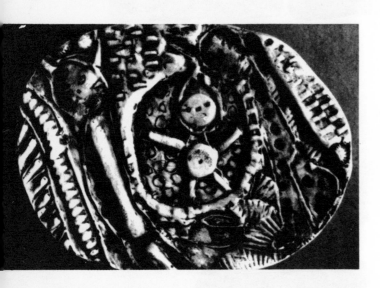

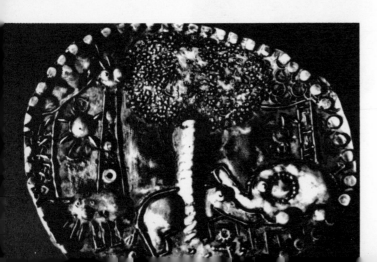

RELIEF SCULPTURE IN CLAY AND PLASTER

Experienced art teachers know that upper-grade children, often self-critical of their graphic ability, need to do something besides draw and paint as a creative outlet. Techniques involving raw materials and new tools whet their expressive appetites, and even though a preliminary drawing is sometimes necessary for a project, the fact that it can be developed in an intriguing and unusual process wins their enthusiastic involvement. Some art activities that belong in this category are metal repoussé reliefs, masks, spoon-mold jewelry, carving, metal enameling, linoleum prints, wire sculpture, papier-mâché, ceramics, and box, toothpick, or reed construction. One project that youngsters respond to, and find success in, is the poured-plaster relief, using either sand or clay as the negative mold.

For this project the following materials and tools are necessary: water-base clay; plaster of Paris; rubber dishpan for mixing plaster; discarded shoe boxes or boxes of similar size and of various shapes; staining colors of either watercolor or oil (neutralized hues); an assortment of sticks and odd instruments, discarded objects of all kinds—nails, screws, bottle caps,

Animals in legend. Plaster of Paris reliefs (grade 4).

forks, dowels, metal screening, round and flat clothes-pins, tongue depressors, reeds, objects from nature such as pine cones and acorns, and a hundred and one throw-away items found in attic, garage, basement, or barn. The clay negative may be modeled on a masonite board or in a shallow box. Because of the convenience, a box is recommended for the elementary child.

The first step in the project is to cut the shoe box down to approximately a three-inch depth and to put a strip of masking tape securely around it, so it will not burst its seams during the process of manipulating the moist clay. The clay itself should be of proper consistency—pliable but not too dry. In some cases the inside of the shoe box may be coated with liquid paraffin to prevent the clay moisture from warping the box, but this is not necessary if the project does not involve too many class periods. The clay should be placed in the box in small balls or pieces and flattened down by hand. If a very flat surface is desired, small pieces of 2 by 4 inch lumber can be used to stamp the clay flat. The clay layer at the bottom of the shoe box should be approximately one inch thick.

Now the fun and problems of designing the relief begin. The teacher will find it helpful to have the students flatten out an apple-sized piece of clay and experiment with the different impressions the assorted tools and objects will make. Through discussion he can bring out the fact that an impression made in the clay will be a bulge or bas-relief in the final plaster cast. Sometimes he can take a quick plaster cast of a student's experiment to show the class what will happen. Knowing the limits and possibilities of the medium frees the student to be more expressive.

There are many possibilities of working the clay negative. A very free approach may utilize fingers, sticks, simple ceramic tools, or nails. Thin snakes of clay may be rolled and applied with clay slip. Strips or shapes may be cut from a thin slab of clay and applied to the clay layer.

One method the teacher will find successful with the children is to limit the design or subject matter to those ideas that can be expressed with the impressions of the "found" objects available. Instead of digging a line into the clay with a nail or stick which produces troublesome excess edges, the child presses his line into the clay, straight lines with popsicle or cotton applicator stick, curved lines with a bent reed, heavy string or cord. What the children enjoy most is the variety of textures and patterns they can achieve through the utilization of the many "found" objects.

Subject matter ideas are unlimited for this technique including imaginative animals and scenes, fish in the sea, a flower garden, birds, self-portraits, or clowns.

Once the composition is attained in clay, the plaster of Paris mix is poured over it to about an inch thickness. Just before the plaster sets, a bent hook or circle of wire can be inserted into it to provide a hanger for the completed relief. The unit on sculpture explains the proper way to mix plaster of Paris. Allow at least a day for the plaster to set. Then the student can pry

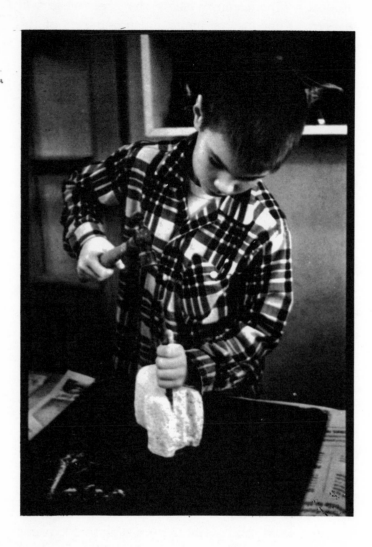

the box open carefully and separate the clay from the plaster. If the child is careful, he may save most of the clay and use it in another project.

Excess edges on the plaster should be scraped or filed off with a knife or rasp. The relief then can be washed with water, using a toothbrush to clean out recessed areas. If the youngster wishes, he can display it in its unembellished form or stain it with diluted oil paint or watercolors in neutral shades such as raw umber, burnt umber, and chrome-oxide green. It is advisable to give the plaster relief a coat of liquid white glue and allow this to dry thoroughly before applying oil stains in order to obtain a subtle surface patina. Coat the completed relief with liquid wax or lacquer to protect the surface.

A similar type of relief can be achieved using moist sand as the negative cast. However, details cannot be delineated as in clay. A number of materials, however, can be embedded in the sand—shells, pieces of glass, or seeds which adhere to the plaster mold when it is removed. Sometimes the sand also sticks to the plaster creating an unusual texture. One other possibility the teacher and youngsters can consider is altering the plaster of Paris mix before pouring with color (dry tempera may be used) or additives such as sand, fine Zonolite, or cement. Remember all these should be mixed with the dry plaster before sifting the mixture into the container of water. Plaster reliefs are definitely a recommended project for the upper-grade child!

SCULPTURE

To introduce a technique into the elementary art program just because it is unique or unusual is often detrimental to the purposes and objectives of art development. If the teacher really believes a new art process is valid and can prove challenging and rewarding to the children if presented in a serious manner, then and only then should it be incorporated in the program. Sculpture in semi-hard materials is one of the projects that has too often been treated in a superficial manner in our schools, with a minimum of emphasis on it as a three-dimensional art form. If the youngsters cannot be allotted enough class time to become thoroughly involved in it, then it should be postponed until they reach the junior-high level. However, if the teacher understands the limitations and possibilities of the sculptural process and the students are properly challenged to tackle the technique and carry it through to its rich culmination, the

Sculptures in plaster of Paris with vermiculite additive (grade 6).

121

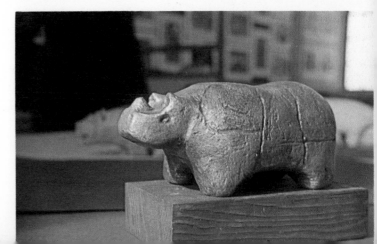

experience can be one of the most rewarding of the young student's life.

Some readily obtainable materials adaptable for elementary sculpture processes are soap, Featherock, firebrick, wax, foamglass, balsa wood, and plaster of Paris molds. Subject matter that can be successfully interpreted by youngsters includes simple forms like fish, birds, animals in repose, heads, and abstractions based on rocks, shells, pebbles, and other biomorphic shapes.

If plaster of Paris is selected as the medium, the plaster should be mixed with additives such as vermiculite or sand in order that the student may sculpt it more readily. The amount of the additive sifted into the plaster determines the porosity and the ease of carving. One part of fine vermiculite to one or two parts of plaster will produce a fairly workable block. A quart or half-gallon wax milk carton or paraffin-coated shoe box will make an adequate mold for casting the blocks.

Students may draw preliminary sketches for their sculpture on paper precut to the size of the block. End, top, and side views should be outlined so that there will be greater understanding of the three-dimensional quality of the sculpture.

While most of the class is engaged in preliminary sketching, the teacher can supervise one or two students at a time in the plaster-molding procedure. At a newspaper-covered worktable or in the sink area all necessary materials should be easily available: plaster of Paris, vermiculite or sand, scoop, mold container, water, rubberized dishpan, spatula, and newspapers to cover the floor and line the wastebaskets. Fill mold container three-quarters full with water. Then pour this water into the rubberized dishpan. Sift the plaster of Paris into the water using hands or a scoop. When islands of plaster appear, add the vermiculite. Stir gently yet swiftly with the hand until thoroughly mixed. When the plaster mixture begins to thicken, pour immediately into a container. Tap the container on a table to remove the trapped air or stir the mixture with a stick. Let it harden overnight and remove the carton. Dry tempera color may be added to the dry plaster for special effects. Avoid brilliant colors. Try subtle colors like siennas, sepias, umbers, and neutral greens.

The student may transfer his profile sketches to the block or draw directly on the mold. When this is done, he files, cuts, or chisels away the excess plaster to delineate the profile view. Next he may use his front or top view sketch and draw these views on the block to determine his next move. He should work slowly and cautiously in removing the excess material. The best tools for this technique are blunt sloyd knives, open plaster rasps, hammers, and chisels. At this stage the youngster should keep turning his sculpture around to define all areas consistently and not overwork one portion to the exclusion of the others.

The teacher should stress fluidity of form and motion; large shapes contrasted against small shapes; an area of emphasis whether it be the feature of animal, the claws of a bird, the horns of a bull, or the eyes of a fish; and finally richness through textures used wisely, effectively, and economically.

Nails, old dental tools, and nut picks are very effective for incising descriptive lines and surface detail. When the basic form or structure has been established and the necessary detail and texture defined, the youngster may give added richness and subtlety to his work through staining, glazing, antiquing, or waxing. As a working surface for the patina, the plaster sculpture should first be coated with a thin layer of white liquid glue. Allow this to dry thoroughly. A coat of walnut wood stain may be applied by using a soft cloth or brush. Rub off excess stain, if necessary, with turpentine. Where the stain did not penetrate through the texture or pattern, re-incise these areas and stain again.

For an unsual and metallic surface quality, the Sculpmetal process is sometimes recommended. Thin down Sculpmetal with Sculpmetal thinner in a small container. Using a stiff bristle brush, apply several thin but even coats to the plaster piece, being careful not to fill in the detailed or incised areas. When the Sculpmetal surface is dry, paint with black India ink. Wait for the ink to dry thoroughly and burnish with steel wool, bringing out all highlights and areas that should be emphasized. For a smooth polished quality, emery paper may be used.

Other stains which work well on precoated plaster are furniture or shoe polishes, and oil paints diluted with turpentine.

Box sculptures (grade 5).

123

BOX SCULPTURE

Older children need changes of pace through new challenges, new materials, new techniques, and new possibilities to keep them interested and engrossed in art.

Box sculpture, like the "found" object constructions in professional art, gives upper-grade youngsters a chance to express their ideas in a three-dimensional form, to manipulate common objects in uncommon ways, to invent unique applications for discarded materials, to struggle with a problem of intricate construction until it is solved, and to really prove the aesthetic axiom that the "whole is greater than the sum of its parts."

Beginning early in the school year, children can be encouraged to bring to class empty boxes of all

Box sculpture (grade 4).

varieties: oatmeal, salt, thumbtack, stationery, tooth-pick, many kinds of mailing tubes, corrugated card-board, and egg cartons. This involvement builds high interest for the project to come. In addition, the fol-lowing "found" objects can be integrated into box construction: wooden beads, wooden clothespins, plastic straws, dowel sticks, toothpicks, corks, paste sticks, sheets and strips of balsa wood, string, and ping-pong balls. All the accumulated boxes and other paraphernalia can be stored in a giant-sized cardboard carton until ready for use. Some tools, equipment, and materials that can contribute to the success of this project are: a vibrating jig saw, coping saw, paper fasteners, pins, masking tape, white glue, rubber cement, scotch tape, gum tape, and tempera. X-acto knives and single-edge razor blades are also useful but must be handled with caution under supervision.

Several specific problems peculiar to this project must be pinpointed and resolved before the class em-barks on this adventure. They involve: storage of materials to be used, storage of work in process, an adequate supply of equipment and tools, and deci-sions on whether to leave the boxes as they are or to paint them. Subject matter possibilities appear limit-less: fantastic figures, spacemen, creatures or animals from another planet, imaginative vehicles, rockets, and toys.

A good way to initiate ideas is to allow the chil-dren a row or table at a time to choose a number of boxes and cardboard tubes (some large, some small) from the general supply, and then manipulate or

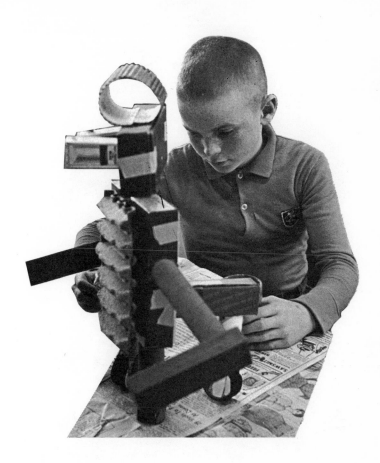

arrange them in different juxtapositions until some structure evolves that triggers a possible sculptural idea. After selecting their basic shapes, the youngsters may want to make preliminary sketches for their constructions. This is an arbitrary procedure. The real excitement and thrill comes from seeing a construction develop and change as new materials are found and added. What might start out as a go-cart can easily emerge metamorphically as a spaceship.

By far the most difficult part of this project is the mechanics involved in fastening the separate boxes together and adding the necessary appendages. Securing one box to another may be done by adhering the two boxes together with a strong glue, using string or large rubber bands to hold the boxes together until the glue sets. Another method of joining is to use masking tape or gum tape, fitting the boxes together, being certain that the tape extends around both boxes being joined. This is especially important when the boxes have a slick surface.

When mailing tubes are used as appendages or joiners, make sure that the hole the child cuts for the tube is slightly smaller than the tube itself. This procedure will provide a tight, stable joint. Balance is very important in this type of construction. If necessary a third leg or support can be created for a standing figure or bird. Sometimes a tail can be used for balancing. In the case of four-footed animals the problem of support is not so crucial.

Interest in the project may be renewed by introducing materials with unusual textural possibilities—

egg cartons for possible armor, corrugated cardboard for decorative relief, and paper or plastic straws for tail or hair.

The success of the project depends in great part on the wealth and variety of boxes and other items brought to class by the students and the teacher. Sometimes an unsual box turns up that looks like the head of a monster and will spark the inspiration for a unique construction.

The decision for or against painting the completed box sculpture is not an easy one. Sometimes the colorfully printed containers create an unusual aesthetic effect when combined, and the youngsters might be challenged to see this new beauty. However, many of the children will want to paint their box sculptures. If so, they will have to make certain technical adjustments. The glossy surfaces of many boxes resist tempera paint, and liquid soap will have to be added to the paint to make it adhere. Another possibility is to paint all the box surfaces with a rubber-base paint and then complete the designs and details in tempera. Sometimes a sgraffito technique may be used by scratching through crayon or paint to the box surface for patterns or textures, or the boxes may be covered with an assortment of pasted newspapers, magazine ads, or colored construction paper scraps.

There are endless exciting possibilities in doing box sculpture. The children and teacher who are brave enough to try it have a real "adventure in art" waiting for them.

Tempera painted masks for a totem pole (grade 2).

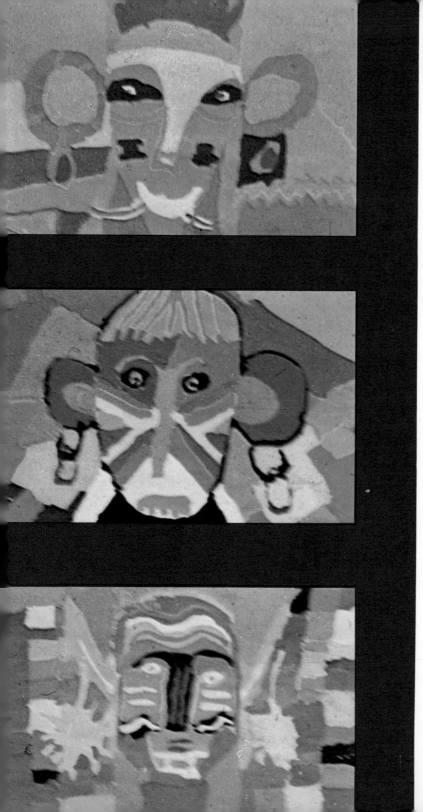

MASKS

Mask making in the elementary schools has been a popular activity but one in which the aesthetic considerations have seldom been fully understood or effectively integrated. Basic design in the allover mask form has often been minimized, and color has been applied in a haphazard, form-negating manner.

The most successful mask structures are usually based on an abstract, restrained, and stylized foundation, rather than a visual rendition, on one which utilizes broad and simple volumes and shapes like the oval, the circle, and the ellipse. All primitive masks of various ethnological groups essentially present a pure and symmetrical design concept of the face of either a man or an animal.

Because of its sophisticated, traditional implications and symbolic connotations, mask making as a project should usually be reserved for the upper elementary grades (5th and 6th), although younger children can often create simple, expressive masks.

A comprehensive study of mask making will reveal certain significant aspects of this art form. Facial features that emphasize the mood or the spirit are exaggerated or distorted. Characteristic elements of the face are never minimized or made to appear as something they are not, such as the triangles for eyes or the stars for the mouth that we see in stereotyped treatments; instead they are imbued with the essence of their particular mood: astonishment, serenity, anger, dignity, reverence, joy, concentration, contem-

Totemic masks done with tempera paint on colored construction paper (grade 2).

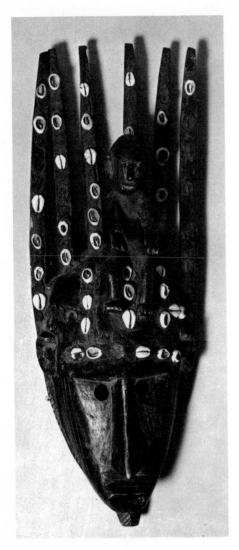

plation, or despair. Symmetrical balance and continuity of forms and features, such as the eyebrow line moving into the nose line, are two of the major characteristics of primitive mask makers. (African masks have inspired countless painters, including Picasso, Matisse, and Amedeo Modigliani.)

Facial decoration can be used to further heighten the mood or spirit of the mask. Students may use lines that repeat and emphasize the dominant features, lines that create texture and pattern on the face, lines that indicate the hair or beard treatment, or combinations of points and lines evolving in limitless pattern possibilities. Color, of course, can enhance or jeopardize the effectiveness of any mask form. It must be integrated with the features, instead of superficially rendered or applied, and must emphasize rather than negate the dominant characteristics. Subtle or limited color schemes or combinations should be encouraged. Bright, vivid colors should be used with discretion. They are especially useful for emphasis and in small amounts provide excellent mood contrast.

LEFT—African mask, University of Iowa Collection. RIGHT —Felt-marker preliminary drawings for plaster gauze mask project (grade 5).

The incentive for mask making in the elementary art program could come just as validly from a study of historical masks, preferably originals if available in the community, as it could from the overworked Halloween themes. Children should be encouraged, too, to make masks as art forms per se, rather than as solely utilitarian objects.

The material and processes most conducive to aesthetic mask making are limited. A clay base is the most effectively controlled process, allowing for highly individual interpretations and for deliberate modeling of features. Another possibility is the application of papier-mâché or plaster-impregnated gauze over a "found" object or common utensil like a dishpan, paper plate, aluminum pie tin, casserole dish, cereal bowl, or beach ball. These forms can be augmented with additional pieces of clay, string, or styrofoam for nose, eyes, mouth, horns, ears, and textures. A common technique is the paper-sculpture method, but it requires much intricate manipulation of paper to achieve simple facial forms. It has many possibilities, however, and can be undertaken in the ordinary classroom because of the availability and simplicity of tools and materials.

For the primary grades the simple, flat mask, paper plate mask, or the totem-pole mask is the best approach since it does not involve a complex three-dimensional technique. American Indians and Indian life are studied by most primary grade children, and this knowledge leads to a rich motivation for many art projects, among them the construction of a group

African mask, Collection of the University of Iowa.

totem pole. Students working individually can paint or crayon animal and human mask faces on assorted colored construction paper, and these can finally be assembled to form a complete totem pole.

White chalk is suggested for the basic sketch of the totem mask since it can be easily erased to allow for corrections or additions that will enhance the design. When the child outlines all the significant features of his mask, be it animal or human being, he then paints or colors the mask to make it come alive. The teacher should suggest that he allow portions of the colored construction paper background to show through and unify his mask composition. He should be encouraged to discover the possibilities of unusual colors to capture the spirit of his mask, to create pattern, to give his mask unity through repetition of a shape, a color, or a design, and to make the important parts of his mask dominant through size, shape, or color.

When his mask is colored, he may make parts of it three-dimensional if he wishes by cutting slits around ears, nose, and horns and folding these out from the main form. When all the children have completed their masks, they are mounted on another sheet of contrasting color, and stapled into cylindrical forms. One form is slipped over an oatmeal box weighted down with sand, and the others telescoped one on top of the other with staples or masking tape to hold them in place. Additional wings, feet, or arms may be constructed by the children out of construction paper, painted, and attached to the totem pole.

Colored construction paper sculpture (grade 4).

131

ESPANA, *color intaglio (32″ x 21″) by Mauricio Lasansky, 1956.*

7

FUNDAMENTAL
ART CONCEPTS
REVIEWED

The classroom teacher of art in the elementary schools today too often possesses a somewhat limited background in art fundamentals. This is not always his fault because in many colleges and universities a double standard for evaluating the creative products of the *fine art* undergraduate and the *art education* major is common, the latter often being treated, unfortunately, as second-class citizens in the art departments. A share of the blame for the sad state of affairs in public school art must fall on the art education instructor who permits his students to settle for less than they are capable of doing, who allows his classes to dissipate valuable time and energy in projects that call for little else than hand-and-eye dexterity or step-by-step manipulation of materials as exemplified in quickie pull-the-strings designs, folded snowflake cut-outs, rice and eggshell mosaics, stereotyped allover patterns or friezes, and preschool level fingerpainting. A similar disservice is forced on the teacher-to-be by the instructor who encourages him to create as a child would, with child-orientated subject matter, so that what often emerges in the teaching of art classes are elves, fawns, and bunny rabbits—everything in fact but the grown-up, mature ideas of the students themselves.

The qualitative art education course in college should provide an integrated and developing contin-

uity between the student's liberal arts preparation, his art history and art studio experiences, and his professional interneship. Valid aesthetic design concepts, based on constant, recurring compositional fundamentals in all the fine arts, past and present, should color and permeate the college program. Its content should be characterized by a deliberate and strong emphasis on expressive drawing and rendering with preliminary drawings and sketches the rule rather than the exception for most studio projects. In essence, inquisitive exploration of environment, continuous exploitation of tools and materials, multisensual approaches in perception, increased visual awareness, self-identification with experience, and empathic, imaginative responses should be stimulated, nurtured, and rewarded.

The college student of art, the interning art teacher, and the veteran teacher of art in the elementary school can learn a great deal if they constantly review and analyze the growing number of publications on art structure and art principles. As they read and research the contemporary material on design and composition, they will discover recurring references to the basic elements of art: point, line, shape, plane, form, value, color, texture, and negative-positive space. They will also find repeated recitations of the fundamental principles: variety, unity, balance, rhythm-repetition, and emphasis. Art, they will discover, is a continually challenging and changing adventure with no shortcuts to the achievement of a satisfying composition or design, and although they

134

TOP—Colored-tissue collage by a college art major in methodology class. CENTER—Linoleum print over colored tissue, a methodology class project by a college art major. BOTTOM—Linoleum print over a magazine ad by a college education major in materials class.

Plaster relief from clay negative mold by art education major.

may borrow inspiration from the past, they must use this knowledge in the contexts of today. The future demands new solutions and new attacks. Yet there are certain guideposts, certain avenues of approach to design and composition which the teacher may wisely utilize to promote his own aesthetic growth, so that he may with confidence help the youngsters in the art class who come to rely on him.

A primary concern of the teacher of art should be an understanding of what sometimes is called *meaningful line*. The line drawing is the nervous system of all composition. Sensitive lines usually vary in weight or emphasis, in opacity and in translucence. They can be subtle, harsh, flowing, static, bold, delicate, furious, calm, or rhythmic. They are sometimes achieved through controlled freedom or spontaneity, sometimes through thoughtful and deliberate action. They may converge, radiate, or intercept one another to create interest, impact, and plastic dimension. An object, shape, or form takes on more visual interest and moves subtly in space when delineated in a variety of sensitive lines. Lines expressively drawn create, define, and delineate shapes, values, and paths of motion. The teacher or his students can never have enough exercise in using line in its myriad ramifications.

A study of pictorial design eventually gets down to the *shape* of things. The shapes created by lines merging, intersecting, or meeting each other take various forms. They may be square, rectangular, complex, round, oval, or amorphous. The creating of

Engravings done on X-ray plates by college art majors in methods class.

expressive shapes or forms in a composition provides the teacher with one of the artist's greatest challenges. Nature is the best source of inspiration as far as variety of shapes is concerned. Natural shapes and forms like those of a tree branch, a rock, a pebble, an animal, a bird, or a man are usually much more sensuous than those based on mathematical formulas. Perhaps this is the reason that artists have usually turned to dilapidated buildings, crumbling wharves, and cluttered interiors for their themes, instead of the clean, antiseptic, and coldly geometric shapes of new buildings, new cars, and new rooms. There is an illusive imperfection about old things that gives them a special aesthetic quality. To clarify this concept a bit more let us refer to a utilitarian object like a Venetian blind. For purposes of function the slats in a blind must have the same dimensions. But when the contemporary artist draws a Venetian blind as part of a composition, he almost always changes the rigid perfection of the rectangular slats to allow for more variety of shape against shape. He may also omit some slats, or he may add more; he may alter the direction of some of them. He is using the artist's poetic license to make his interpretation of the Venetian blind more pictorial and more expressive. There is far too much reliance on geometric, mathematical perfection in the delineation of table tops, windows, doors, cabinets, utensils, and other man-made articles. The teacher should turn often to a study of nature's varied forms when his own inventiveness in evolving interesting shapes lags.

The shapes of things, objects, trees, animals, people, and buildings in a composition are sometimes called positive shapes. The areas left round them are sometimes referred to as negative shapes, even though the negative shape may also define the sky, the ground, the water, or the atmosphere. In any case where the positive shapes are varied in size and form, the negative shapes also gain variety and excitement. When a composition is pictorially effective and exciting, it is usually in *good shape*.

The element of *value* plays an important role in the visual arts. Value, simply stated, refers to the light or dark factors in a design or composition. Every shade and tint of every color has a place on the value scale, and teachers of art must learn to see color in terms of value. Value studies of great works of art will help the teacher understand dark and light composition and juxtaposition. The value range of any composition can be sharp or definite, blurred or subtle, depending on the mood of the expression or interpretation. Sharply contrasting values indicate exciting, highly charged, and dramatic compositions. Subtle value relationships provide tranquil, calm, and more unified themes. Value can be utilized, too, to create movement in a painting and to lead the viewer from one area to another.

Color in painting is a real headache to art students, to teachers of art, and even to professional artists. It is not uncommon to see an art student give an excellent account of himself in a black and white drawing, yet probe the depths of frustration when he

Tempera paint and India ink batik made in methodology class by a college art major.

tackles color. All the color theories, color wheels, and color harmonies in existence cannot help him in his dilemma. For example, what for years some color theorists have labeled *cool colors,* others now call *warm colors.* What were once identified as receding colors are now termed advancing colors. Colors that never should be together according to the traditionalists of the thirties now keep company in a togetherness undreamed of. The artists Matisse, Paul Gauguin, Raoul Dufy, Picasso, and Hans Hofmann are acclaimed pioneers in liberating the academies from color stereotypes and color restrictions. *Today anything goes in color—if it succeeds.*

To the teacher of art this may indicate chaos and confusion in the realm of color orientation. However, all is not lost. There are some concepts, some practices that can lead a student to an understanding of color, to its limitations, and its possibilities.

In most colleges the painting instructors still suggest a palette of colors for the student, and although this palette varies from school to school, it is similar in one important respect. It is usually a *limited* palette. Limitation, therefore, plays an important role in the mastery of color composition. To play it safe, the art student or art teacher might limit his painting to black, gray, white, and one color, or to all the tints and shades of one color, sometimes referred to as a monochromatic scheme. A more complex yet controlled interpretation involves the use of an analogous color range, those colors adjacent to each other on the color wheel.

TOP—Actual scene chosen as the subject of a collage. CENTER—The scene as sketched by Ted Ramsay. BOTTOM—The completed collage by Ted Ramsay.

To avoid the pitfalls of clashing colors and strident chromatic relationships, many art instructors recommend minimizing the intensity of colors used in a compositon. This process sometimes called neutralization or dulling of a color involves the mixing of complements or colors that are opposite each other on the color wheel. Many colors already available in tempera, oil, or watercolor are already neutralized, for example, sepia, sienna, raw umber, brown, Hooker's green, and green gold. Another suggestion offered by studio instructors to give unity or coherence to a painting is to mix a little of one basic color with every other color utilized. This, in essence, is another kind of neutralization. Still another avenue to unity in color composition is glazing. One color thinned down with water, turpentine, or some other dilutent is applied over the painting imbuing it with a consistent tonality.

Even though many of the old theories have been thrown into a cocked hat, some gentle persuasions in color orchestration persist. A little bit of a bright, intense color goes a long way in a chromatic composition that is basically neutral. Colors can be repeated to create unity and movement. Dark or cool colors often recede; bright or warm colors usually advance. Complementary colors like red and green in their full intensity create jarring contrasts. Black, white, and gray can be used with any color combination without creating tangible color conflicts. Often they may add the sparkle of sharp definition to a design. The teacher must always be aware that the character and

TOP—Crayon engraving with Craypas overlay, a methodology class project by a college art major. CENTER—Collage of "found materials" by a college art major in methodology class. BOTTOM—Mixed media painting by a college art major in methodology class.

139

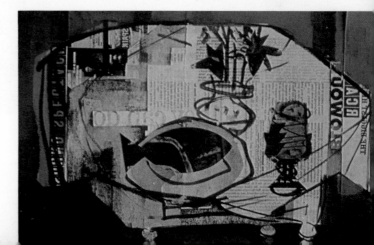

impact of color depends primarily on the colors around it—a green shape on a turquoise background may be relatively unnoticed, but a bright red spot against a bright green background will vibrate and arrest the eye.

The painters of the post-impressionistic and expressionist era, Gauguin, Vincent Van Gogh, Franz Marc, Karl Schmidt-Rottluff, and Matisse, have provided us with a whole new approach to color. No longer do artists rely on the use of local color which only captures the natural or real appearance of an object, figure, or place. A personal, subjective interpretation of color is now the painter's goal. The unique result is blue cows, green people, or purple turtles. The painting takes on a new reality, a color integrity of its own.

The teacher who wishes to learn more about color possibilities must study the paintings of the impressionists, the post-impressionists, and the expressionists, as well as the diverse and sometimes shocking color orchestrations of today. He should not forget in his color research the luminous stained glass windows of the Gothic period, the jewel-like miniatures of the Far East, the frescoes of the Renaissance, the mosaics of Byzantium, or the ukiyoye color woodcuts of Japan.

When we analyze *space* in composition or design, we often confuse the young student. In two-dimensional works, space is sometimes considered the empty area between objects in the painting. This kind of space is commonly known as decorative or flat space.

In this same vein, negative (nonobject) space and positive (object) space are also important factors.

Another category we must deal with is space-in-depth, often described as plastic space. Common pictorial devices for achieving the illusion of space-in-depth on a two-dimensional plane include diminishing size of objects, sharp and clear details in the foreground, blurred indistinct elements in the background, overlapping shapes or forms, intense colors in the foreground, neutral, grayed colors in the distance, and utilization of time-honored perspective systems of vanishing points, horizon lines, and converging parallels.

The art teacher should remember that the decorative or shallow exploitation of space, in which the picture plane is respected, is a natural one for young children. The more objects or things they put into their pictures, the more intricate and exciting their nonobject space usually becomes. As the children grow older they discover pictorial space through overlapping, through diminishing forms, and through converging lines. Much of this knowledge comes intuitively, but some awareness of space recognition can be stimulated. The laws or rules of perspective should not be imposed on a child unless he indicates a need for them. One cannot insure the success of a composition by utilizing the canons of perspective, for too often the dependence on perspective formulas leads to sterility in expression. Some of the greatest painters in the world ignored the visual limitations demanded by perspective. In some instances students

Linoleum print made over a newspaper ad in materials class by a college education major.

ASSEMBLY OF PAST POLAR EXPLORERS, *encaustic (48" x 60")* *by Byron Burford, Edmondson Collection, Des Moines Art Center.*

jeopardize the aesthetic character of their compositions by relying too rigidly on natural lighting and on shadows to create solid forms in space. The teacher should encourage them to explore other interpretations than those based on natural laws and effects.

An indispensable avenue to pictorial expression is the effective exploitation of *balance* or *symmetry.* Most teachers are familiar with the two types of balance: symmetrical or formal and asymmetrical or informal. Much of the painting of the Western world up to the late 19th century and the artistic output of the Middle and Far East adhered to the rather formalized or symmetrical disciplines of composition (though there were some notable exceptions among the great artists like Rembrandt, Pieter Brueghel, Rubens, and Francisco Goya who moved from one symmetry to another as the composition demanded). Since Paul Cézanne's day, artists have for the most part eschewed the rigid formulas of symmetrical orchestration or juxtaposition.

Purely formalized compositions usually lack that open-ended orchestration and variety which permits the observer to make his own personal tours and explorations of a painting, each time discovering some new avenue of approach to the work, some subtle emphasis, or some hidden revelation and beauty.

A common misconception engaged in by some teachers of elementary art is that if the child draws something very large and puts it in the center of the picture, it immediately creates emphasis or draws attention. Placement in the composition alone *does not insure either domination or subordination.* Other factors must be considered. If the object or figure in the middle of the page is simple in form, if it is subdued in color, if it is lacking in detail, texture, or pattern, if the areas surrounding it are similar in color and value, then in all probability it will attract no more attention than a similarly rendered object or figure on the periphery of the composition. To gain emphasis in a picture an object must have other attributes than centricity per se. It must have, in fact, eccentricity.

Despite the reminder that there are no hard and fast rules in pictorial design, art students and art teachers usually find that their visual expressions gain more flexibility, more adjustability when they do not put the main motif or figure of their painting exactly in the center of the picture plane. As we study and analyze the works of contemporary painters and printmakers, we are made aware of the psychological, asymmetrical balance that artists use. Although, at first glance, the main figure or form appears formally centered, a second closer investigation indicates a subtle off-balance. In some instances where the main object dominates the composition centrally, as in the case of a vase of flowers, a tree, or a portrait, the break-up of negative space on each side of the central axis is planned or composed so effectively that centricity is no handicap.

Variety or diversity plays a very important role in the structure of the fine arts. The study of the recurrence of the principle of variety in the great works of art, past and present, is of inestimable value in the teacher's aesthetic development. Analyses of masterpieces of painting and printmaking reveal the constant utilization of a variety of subtle shapes, with seldom two shapes, planes, or spaces exactly alike.

Nature and the elements can provide and inspire us with multiple instances of unusual variety: the ice breaking on a river, the patterns of clouds, the branches or roots of a tree, the crystals in snowflakes, the cracks in mud flats, oil flowing on water, erosion in soil, snowdrift patterns, and thousands of microscopic revelations of natural substances. Though man is nature's child, he must learn to consciously define and employ variety in his visual expressions. Too often the shapes he creates are monotonous, mathematically rigid, conforming, and stereotyped. He could do well to look once more upon the stripes of a zebra, the spots on a leopard, the wings of a butterfly, the shell of a turtle, and the frost on the windowpane.

Variety as a force in pictorial design can be exploited in many ways and in many instances. It can be applied to every element of the composition—line, shape, value, color, texture—to give heterogeneity and sparkle to a painting, but it must be counterbalanced by a repetition of these same elements if unity is to be achieved. Emphasis, too, must be considered, and also subordination. The principle of variety can help us in the placement of objects, figures, or shapes in our composition—things may rest

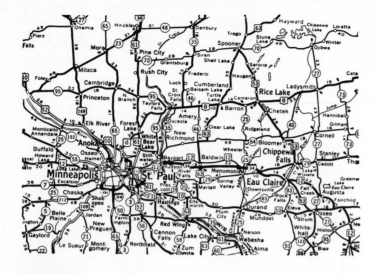

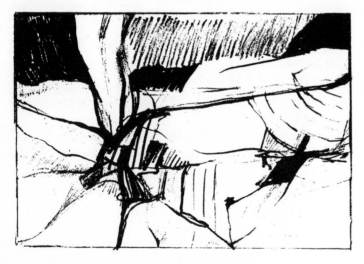

A road map and a unified composition suggest many analogies.

on different levels—things may stop at different levels —objects or shapes may be different sizes and create different negative spaces between them.

The complete, unified composition in which diverse shapes, colors, values, and texture are incorporated or fused into an ordered and satisfying whole should be the goal of artists, art teachers, and art students. In too many instances objects or figures are rendered in isolation and treated only as separate vignettes (and here we are not dealing with preliminary sketches as such). The figure, the vase, the bird, or the cabin is insulated in the middle of the page with no indications of planned spatial or environmental relationships. This kind of disjointed effect can often be solved through the use of subordinated and overlapping shapes, through the exploitation of varied positions and sizes of the same figure or object, through the utilization of related and subtle backgrounds, or through the wise use of complementary environmental aspects that relate to the main theme. All these avenues should be explored by the student.

One effective method of achieving organic unity in a composition is based on the analogy that "a good painting is like a road map." As in a map, the eye moves along the composition's main highways or arterials with subordinate sallies along county roads. Geographic areas, created by connecting and bisecting routes in a map, can be compared to the unusual amorphic shapes often found in abstract, nonobjective, or expressionistic paintings.

The observer enters the painting (map) at one of many possible inroads, then is led to a major interstate highway that carries him to a point of emphasis or center of interest. Other subordinate routes (lines) radiate or disperse from this focal spot to less important areas. The more complex the painting, the more routes in and out of the composition are provided, and to make the challenge complete, the observer may choose a different approach each time he comes to view the picture.

In this age of jets and rockets, it is perhaps common for us to be caught up in the rush of things. Perhaps that is why so many art students skim through their work and why instant, facile nonobjective painting appeals to them. Much of what one sees in art today requires only a minimum of effort. We are misled if we equate speed of execution with freedom of expression. A quality or mood of spontaneity in a work of art is usually attained through thoughtful, controlled, and deliberate action. It is the result of many hours, many years of mastering a technique, of ordering the vision, and of integrating mind, heart, and hand.

The basic tenets in this chapter are not new, nor are they revolutionary. We believe that they help to establish a workable foundation for the art teacher. There will always be the exception to the rule, but in most instances and in most classrooms, a fundamentals approach, based on a sound understanding of aesthetic quality, can prove to be the most stabilizing and significant.

TOP—Colored chalk drawing on colored construction paper combined with a tempera paint spatter over selected leaves by a college education major in materials class. CENTER—Colored chalk drawing on colored construction paper by a college education major. BOTTOM—Multi-crayon engraving by a college art major in methodology class.

appendix

A

THE CHILD: HIS CHARACTERISTICS

THE FIRST AND SECOND GRADER:

Is naturally active and easily excited
Likes to work with his hands
Has a strong feeling of possessiveness
Is eager to learn NO
Wants to be first
Has a limited span of interest and is easily fatigued
Takes great pride in his work NO
Has feelings that are easily hurt
Is alternately cooperative and uncooperative
Can usually grasp only one idea at a time
Delights in imaginative games and stories
Desires the approval of teacher and classmates sometimes

TOP LEFT—Wet-storage facility. BOTTOM LEFT—Tote-tray facility. TOP RIGHT—Tempera-paint facility. CENTER, BOTTOM RIGHT—Children's art exhibit.

Still lives in his own secret world
- Is interested in new things to touch and taste
- Is interested in moving and mechanical devices
- Enjoys games, television, family outings, and illustrated books
- Likes to pretend and play make-believe
- Is an individual in his efforts

THE THIRD AND FOURTH GRADER:

Has improved eye-hand coordination

Has better command of small muscles

Is becoming aware of the differences in people

Begins to set standards for himself

Is learning to be responsible, orderly, and cooperative

Forms separate sex groups

Sometimes joins gangs and coteries

Enjoys comics, magazines, and travel

Is growing in self-evaluation and evaluation of others

Is able to concentrate for a longer period of time

Is developing a sense of humor

Is interested in the life processes of plants and animals and in many diverse aspects of nature

Develops a strong interest in sports and hobbies

THE FIFTH AND SIXTH GRADER:

Is developing a strong sense of right and wrong

Concentrates more on individual interests

Is interested in varied activities depending on his or her sex

Is becoming more dependable, responsible, and reasonable

Is interested in perfection and needs helpful guidance

Develops interests outside of school—in the community and the world of man

Often criticizes grown-ups

Develops an increasing interest and working span

Varies in maturity—girls are often more mature than boys

Develops interests in collections and in exchanging things

Begins a phase of hero-worship

Is self-conscious and self-critical

Enjoys working in groups

Is undergoing critical emotional and physical changes

B

THE CHILD: HIS NATURAL DEVELOPMENT IN ART

Knowing what the child is like, his interests, his needs, and his eccentricities, is very important indeed for the competent art teacher, but another area of knowledge is just as crucial for the encouragement of the child's creative growth, and that is an understanding of what children can do *naturally* in visual interpretation. Here again the graphic potential and the complexity of the imagery varies with the stages of the child's physical, mental, and social development. Some children may have had experiences at home in working with art materials; others may have had limited opportunities. Some may have developed a very keen interest in some particular phase of their environment such as horses, trains, plants, or birds, and their observations will often distinguish their art work from others in the class because of eidetic and perceptual ability. Since children express best what they are most sensitive to, or affected by, it is often possible for the discerning teacher to discover what they know about their world, and what their attitudes and feelings may be.

My Family at Home, *developmental drawing (grade 1)*.

THE FIRST GRADER MAY:

Continue to use the geometric symbols (line, square, rectangle, and triangle) which he used in kindergarten, but may alter the form of these symbols as he reacts to new experiences

Use a basic symbol, such as a circle, to represent several ideas—the sun, the human or animal head, a table, a flower, an apple, a lamp, or a tree top

Devise many possible variations for a figure, a house, a tree, a dog, or a truck

Repeat the symbols he has mastered over and over again

Use symbols that are often different from any used by others in the class

Simplify his concepts and may not always be concerned with details

Draw things as he knows and feels them to be, for example, the band of sky at the top of the page, the sun that dominates almost every picture, the railroad tracks that never converge

Draw things larger that are important to him, minimize or omit things that are not essential to his idea

Begin to draw related objects on a baseline which may be at the bottom of the page itself or a line drawn slightly above it

Use color in a personal, imaginative, or emotional way without regard to its identification in nature

MY FAMILY AT HOME, *developmental drawing (grade 2).*

THE SECOND GRADER MAY:

Change subtly from geometric, symbolic interpretation to more specific characterization

Begin to use more details in his pictures—hair,
buttons, belts, eyebrows, glasses, shoelaces,
curtains, patterns in clothes, and buildings

Sometimes show both inside and outside of a
building in an X-ray manner

Often depict related events of an experience in a
time-sequence record

Introduce more than one base line in his picture
to show distant but related happenings

Use an unusual fold-over method to show shop-
pers on both sides of the street, people around
a table or swimming pool, or players on a
baseball diamond

Use characteristic details to show differentiation
between sexes

Draw distant objects the same size as those
nearer but may place them higher on the page

Sometimes draw objects to show completeness,
such as a tilted table top and four legs, or a
house showing front and two full sides

Use color more naturalistically but still does not
distinguish between different greens in plants
and leaves or the various tonalities of sky,
water, and earth

THE THIRD AND FOURTH GRADER MAY:

Begin to draw with more conscious planning, *Not so*, *IN Grant.* utilizing more realistic proportions

Create space through overlapping of forms *yes*

Select and arrange objects with predetermined effects in mind and fill space in terms of purpose

Move the baseline up to become the horizon line *no*

Draw distant objects smaller as well as higher on the page *some*

Sometimes show several points of view in one picture—a bird's-eye view combined with a natural, eye-level view *no*

Make brave efforts to show action in drawing people and animals but is often handicapped by his misunderstanding of proportion and foreshortening *yes*

My Family at Home, *developmental drawings.* TOP—
Grade 3. BOTTOM—Grade 4.

THE FIFTH AND SIXTH GRADER MAY:

Become increasingly so critical of his own results and become so discouraged with his efforts that he may start to lose interest in art activities unless wisely challenged, guided, and motivated

Develop a growing curiosity to experiment with varied materials, tools, and complex processes

Become interested in his environment as a source for his drawings and paintings

Sometimes use shading to make forms appear solid and round

Experiment with dark and light patterns in his pictures and with a variety of textural effects

Begin to use rudimentary perspective principles in drawing houses, streets, sidewalks, fences, and roads

Choose subject matter for art which is related to human interests and activities, community and world events, and current affairs in science and space exploration

MY FAMILY AT HOME, *developmental drawings.* TOP—Grade 5 BOTTOM—Grade 6.

C

RECOMMENDED REFERENCE BOOKS, BULLETINS, AND PERIODICALS

BOOKS FOR CHILDREN

The letters following each reference indicate those suitable for use in the primary grades (P), those which may be used in the upper grades (U), and those appropriate for all grades (A).

Ames, Gerald, and Wyler, Rose. *Giant Golden Book of Biology,* illustrated by Charles Harper. New York: Golden Press, Inc., 1961. **(U)**

Bate, Norman. *When Cavemen Painted.* New York: Charles Scribner's Sons, 1963. **(A)**

Baumann, Hans. *The Caves of the Great Hunters.* New York: Pantheon Books, 1954. **(U)**

Borten, Helen. *Do You See What I See?* New York: Simon & Shuster, 1951. **(P)**

Browner, Richard. *Look Again!* New York: Atheneum Publishers, Inc., 1962. (P)

Candy, Robert. *Nature Notebook.* Boston: Houghton Mifflin Co., 1962. (U)

Chase, Alice Elizabeth. *Famous Paintings.* New York: Platt and Munk, 1962. (U)

Fenton, Carrol L., and Fenton, Mildred A. *In Prehistoric Seas.* Garden City, N. Y.: Doubleday and Co., Inc., 1963. (A)

Gibson, Katharine. *More Pictures to Grow Up With.* New York: Studio Publications, Inc., 1946. (A)

———. *Pictures to Grow Up With.* New York: Studio Publications, Inc., 1942. (A)

———. *Pictures by Young Americans.* New York: Oxford University Press, 1946. (U)

Gill, Bob. *What Color Is Your World?* New York: Iyan Obolensky, Inc., 1963. (A)

Gilliard, E. Thomas. *Living Birds of the World.* Garden City, N. Y.: Doubleday and Company, Inc., 1958. (A)

Glubok, Shirley. *The Art of Ancient Egypt.* New York: Atheneum Publishers, Inc., 1963.

Hammond, Penny, and Thomas, Katrina. *My Skyscraper City.* Garden City, N. Y.: Doubleday and Company, Inc., 1963. (A)

Hay, John, and Strong, Arline. *A Sense of Nature.* Garden City, N. Y.: Doubleday and Company, Inc., 1962. (U)

Herald, Earl S. *Living Fishes of the World.* Garden City, N. Y.: Doubleday and Company, Inc., 1961. (A)

Holme, Bryan. *Pictures to Live With.* New York: The Viking Press, 1959. (U)

Janson, H. W., and Janson, D. J. *The Story of Painting for Young People.* New York: Harry N. Abrams, Inc., 1963. (U)

Kablo, Martin. *World of Color.* New York: McGraw-Hill Book Company, 1963. (P)

Kessler, Leonard. *Art Is Everywhere.* New York: Dodd, Mead and Co., 1958. (U)

———. *The Worm, the Bird and You.* New York: Dodd, Mead and Co., 1962. (A)

———. *What's in a Line?* New York: William R. Scott, Inc., 1961. (A)

Kirn, Ann. *Full of Wonder.* New York: The World Publishing Co., 1959. (A)

Klots, A. B., and Klots, E. B. *Living Insects of the World.* Garden City, N. Y.: Doubleday and Co., Inc., 1959. (A)

Krauss, Ruth. *A Hole is to Dig.* New York: Harper and Brothers, 1952. (P)

Low, Joseph. *Adam's Book of Odd Creatures.* New York: Atheneum Publishers, Inc., 1962. (A)

Munari, Bruno. *Bruno Munari's Zoo.* Cleveland, Ohio: The World Publishing Co., 1963. (P)

Munro, Eleanor C. *The Golden Encyclopedia of Art.* New York: Golden Press, Inc., 1961. (U)

O'Neill, Mary. *Hailstones and Halibut Bones.* Garden City, N. Y.: Doubleday and Company, Inc., 1961. (A)

Ross, Edward. *Insects Close Up.* Berkeley, Calif.: University of California Press, 1953. (A)

Sanderson, Ivan T. *Living Mammals of the World.* Garden City, N. Y.: Hanover House, 1955. (A)

Scheele, E. Wilham. *Prehistoric Animals.* New York: The World Publishing Co., 1954. (U)

Schlein, Miriam. *Shapes.* New York: William Scott, Inc., 1958. (P)

Smith, William Jay. *What Did I See?* New York: Crowell-Collier Press, 1962. (P)

Strache, Wolf. *Forms and Patterns in Nature.* New York: Pantheon Books, Inc., 1956. Superb black and white photographs. (A)

Weisgard, Leonard. *Treasures to See.* New York: Harcourt, Brace and Co., 1956. (U)

Wolff, Janet, and Owett, Bernard. *Let's Imagine Colors.* New York: E. P. Dutton and Co., 1963. (A)

BOOKS ON ART EDUCATION

Barkan, Manuel. *Through Art to Creativity.* Boston: Allyn and Bacon, Inc., 1960. Analysis and evaluation of art activities in a number of self-contained classrooms. Sessions tape-recorded and photographed by the author.

Bealmer, William, and Committee. *Children Learn and Grow Through Art Experiences.* Springfield, Ill.: Office of Supt. of Public Instruction, State of Illinois, 1958. An excellent resource guide for the teacher of elementary art.

Cole, Natalie R. *The Arts in the Classroom.* New York: The John Day Co., Inc., 1942.

Conant, Howard, and Randall, Arne. *Art In Education.* Peoria, Ill.: Chas. A. Bennett Co., Inc., 1959. Effective report on the art teacher's characteristics and professional preparation. Excellent study on the exceptional child.

D'Amico, Victor. *Creative Teaching in Art,* rev. ed. Scranton, Pa.: International Textbook Co., 1960.

de Francesco, Italo L. *Art Education: Its Means and Ends.* New York: Harper and Brothers, 1958. A comprehensive examination of the complex and total responsibility of art education in our schools. Especially worthwhile are the philosophical and theoretical concepts which are presented in a manner that gives meaning and objectivity to the teaching of art.

Erdt, Margaret Hamilton. *Teaching Art in the Elementary School,* rev. ed. New York: Holt, Rinehart & Winston, Inc., 1962. Chapter II, "Thinking through an Art Experience," emphasizes the teacher's contribution in a positive way. Very good reference material listed at close of each chapter.

Fearing, Kelly, Martin, Clyde, and Beard, Evelyn. *Our Expanding Vision.* Austin, Tex.: W. S. Benson Co., 1960. A series of graded paperback books recommended to widen the art horizons of children anywhere.

Gaitskell, Charles D. *Children and Their Art.* New York: Harcourt Brace and Co., 1958. Part I, "Preparing to Teach Art," presents theoretical practices and contemporary purposes in art education in a lucid and forthright manner.

Hoover, Louis F. *Art Activities for the Very Young.* Worcester, Mass.: Davis Publications, Inc., 1961.

Jefferson, Blanche. *Teaching Art to Children.* Boston: Allyn and Bacon, Inc., 1959. Analyzes some diverse methods of teaching elementary art.

Keiler, Manfred. *The Art of Teaching Art.* Lincoln, Neb.: University of Nebraska Press, 1961. Although aimed primarily at the secondary school art teacher, this text has a worthwhile message for any teacher of art. It is blunt, straight-forward and unequivocal in its philosophy of art education. Read Part I, "Aims and Concepts."

Knudsen, Estelle, and Christensen, Ethel. *Children's Art Education.* Peoria, Ill.: Chas. A. Bennett Co., Inc., 1957.

Linderman, Earl W., and Heberholz, Donald W. *Developing Artistic and Perceptual Awareness.* Dubuque, Iowa: Wm. C. Brown Company, 1964.

Logan, Fred M. *Growth of Art in American Schools.* New York: Harper and Brothers, 1955. An authoritative and comprehensive historical survey of art education in the United States.

Lowenfeld, Viktor. *Creative and Mental Growth,* 3rd ed. New York: The Macmillan Co., 1957. For a study of the child's *natural* development in graphic expression and how his physical, social, and emotional growth affects his art, this text has no peer.

Manzella, David. *Educationists and the Evisceration of the Visual Arts.* Scranton, Pa.: International Textbook Co., 1963. A literate exposé of antithetical art education practices in American schools, coupled with an appeal for reforms.

Mattil, Edward L. *Meaning in Crafts.* Englewood Cliffs, N. J.: Prentice-Hall, Inc., 1959.

McFee, June King. *Preparation for Art.* San Francisco, Calif.: Wadsworth Publishing Co., Inc., 1961. A discerning text that relates psychological, anthropological, and sociological principles in presenting an approach to art education.

McIlvain, Dorothy S. *Art for the Primary Grades.* New York: G. P. Putnam's Sons, 1961. Limited to the kindergarten and grades 1, 2, 3. Detailed descriptions of a variety of projects. Appendix on materials should be noted.

Mendelowitz, Daniel M. *Children Are Artists.* Stanford, Calif.: Stanford University Press, 1963.

Merritt, Helen. *Guiding Free Expression in Children's Art.* New York: Holt, Rinehart & Winston, Inc., 1964.

Parkhurst, Helen H. *Exploring the Child's World.* New York: Appleton-Century-Crofts, Inc., 1951.

Randall, Arne W. *Murals for Schools.* Worcester, Mass.: Davis Press, Inc., 1962. Well annotated descriptions of the many possible techniques for mural making.

Randall, Arne W., and Halvorsen, Ruth E. *Painting in the Classroom.* Worcester, Mass.: Davis Publications, Inc., 1963.

Read, Herbert E. *Education Through Art.* New York: Pantheon Books, Inc., 1949.

Trucksess, Fran. *Creative Art: Elementary Grades.* Boulder, Colo.: Pruett Press, Inc., 1962.

Wickiser, Ralph L. *An Introduction to Art Education.* Yonkers-on-Hudson, N. Y.: World Book Co., 1957. Especially recommended for the substance of Chapter 2, "Investigating the Nature of the Art Experience."

BOOKS ON ART

Anderson, Donald M. *Elements of Design.* New York: Holt, Rinehart & Winston, Inc., 1961.

Bethers, Ray. *How Paintings Happen.* New York: Norton Publishers, 1951.

————. *Composition in Pictures.* New York: Pitman Publishing Corp., 1956.

Canaday, John. *Keys to Art.* New York: Tudor Publishing Co., 1963.

Downer, Marion. *Discovering Design.* New York: Lothrop, Lee and Shepard Co., 1947.

————. *The Story of Design.* New York: Lothrop, Lee and Shepard Co., 1963.

Emerson, Sybil. *Design: A Creative Approach.* Scranton, Pa.: International Textbook Co., 1953.

Faulkner, R., Ziegfeld, E., and Hill, G. *Art Today,* rev. ed. New York: Holt, Rinehart & Winston, Inc., 1963.

Kuh, Katherine. *Art Has Many Faces.* New York: Harper and Brothers, 1951.

————. *The Artist's Voice.* New York: Harper and Brothers, 1962.

Levi, Julian. *Modern Art: An Introduction* (paperback). New York: Pitman Publishing Corp., 1961.

Ocvirk, Otto G., Bone, Robert, Stinson, Robert, and Wigg, Philip. *Art Fundamentals: Theory and Practice.* Dubuque, Iowa: Wm. C. Brown Co., 1960. An excellent text for the teacher for study or review of basic art fundamentals.

Read, Herbert. *The Meaning of Art.* New York: Pitman Publishing Corp., 1951.

Riley, Olive. *Masks and Magic.* New York: Studio Publications, 1955.

Schinneller, James A. *Art: Search and Self-Discovery.* Scranton, Pa.: International Textbook Co., 1961. Although not dealing specifically with the elementary art program, this text, because it enriches and expands the reader's art awareness, should be on the elementary art teacher's reading list.

Seiberling, Frank. *Looking into Art.* New York: Henry Holt and Co., Inc., 1959.

Sternberg, Harry. *Composition: Anatomy of Picture Making* (paperback). New York: Pitman Publishing Corp., 1958.

————. *Realistic, Abstract Art* (paperback). New York: Pitman Publishing Corp., 1959.

Wedd, J. A. Dunkin. *Pattern and Texture: Sources of Design.* New York: Studio Publications, 1946.

BOOKS ON TECHNIQUES

Albert, Calvin, and Seckler, Dorothy. *Figure Drawing Comes to Life.* New York: Reinhold Publishing Corp., 1962.

Aller, Doris, and Aller, Diane. *Mosaics.* Menlo Park, Colo.: Lane Book Co., 1960.

Andrews, Michael F. *Creative Printmaking.* Englewood Cliffs, N. J.: Prentice-Hall, Inc., 1963.

Argiro, Larry. *Mosaic Art Today.* Scranton, Pa.: International Textbook Co., 1961.

Baranski, Matthew. *Graphic Design.* Scranton, Pa.: International Textbook Co., 1960.

Barford, George. *Clay in the Classroom.* Worcester, Mass.: Davis Publications, Inc., 1963.

Brow, Francis. *Collage.* New York: Pitman Publishing Corp., 1963.

Cataldo, John W. *Lettering: A Guide for Teachers.* Worcester, Mass.: Davis Publications, Inc., 1958.

Daingerfield, Marjorie. *Fun and Fundamentals of Sculpture.* New York: Charles Scribner's Sons, 1963.

Dhaemers, Robert, and Slatoff, Howard A. *Simple Jewelry Making for the Classroom.* San Francisco, Calif.: Fearon Publishers, 1958.

Dobkin, Alexander. *Principles of Figure Drawing.* Cleveland, Ohio: World Publishing Co., 1948.

Guild, Vera P. *Creative Use of Stitches.* Worcester, Mass.: Davis Publications, Inc., 1964.

Heller, Jules. *Printmaking Today.* New York: Henry Holt and Co., 1958.

Horn, George. *Bulletin Boards.* New York: Reinhold Publishing Corp., 1962.

Johnson, Pauline. *Creating with Paper.* Seattle, Wash.: University of Washington Press, 1958.

Karasz, Mariska. *Adventure in Stitches.* New York: Funk and Wagnalls Co., 1959.

Krevitsky, Nik. *Batik—Art and Craft.* New York: Reinhold Publishing Corporation, 1964.

Kuwabara, Minoru, Hayashi, Kenzo, and Kumamoto, Takanori. *Cut and Paste.* New York: Ivan Obolensky, Inc., 1961.

Lynch, John. *How to Make Collages.* New York: Viking Press, 1961.

————. *Metal Sculpture.* New York: Studio Crowell, 1957.

————. *Mobile Design.* New York: Studio Crowell, 1955.

Magdalen, Mary I.H.M. Sister. *Mosaics for Everyone.* Los Angeles, Calif.: Brown Letter Shop, 1958.

Marks, Mickey Klar. *Sand Sculpturing.* New York: Dial Junior Books, Inc., 1962.

Mayer, Ralph. *Artist's Handbook of Materials and Techniques,* rev. ed. New York: Viking Press, 1958.

Nelson, Glenn C. *Ceramics.* New York: Holt, Rinehart and Winston, Inc., 1960.

Nicholaïdes, Kimon. *The Natural Way to Draw.* Boston: Houghton Mifflin Co., 1941.

Ota, Koshi, Kakehi, Susumu, Haba, Tokuzo, Baba, Kiyoaki, and Fukita, Bummei. *Printing for Fun.* New York: McDowell, Obolensky, 1960.

Peterdi, Gabor. *Printmaking.* New York: The Macmillan Co., 1959.

Randall, Reino, and Haines, Edward C. *Bulletin Boards and Display.* Worcester, Mass.: Davis Publications, Inc., 1961.

Rasmusen, Henry. *Printmaking with Monotype.* New York: Chilton Publishing Co., 1960.

Röttger, Ernst. *Creative Clay Design.* New York: Reinhold Publishing Corp., 1963.

————. *Creative Paper Design.* New York: Reinhold Publishing Corp., 1961.

————. *Creative Wood Design.* New York: Reinhold Publishing Corp., 1961.

Simon, Howard. *Primer of Drawing,* rev. ed. New York: Sterling Publishing Co., Inc., 1958.

Sternberg, Harry. *Woodcut.* New York: Pitman Publishing Corp., 1962.

Struppeck, Jules. *Creation of Sculpture.* New York: Henry Holt and Co., 1952.

Untracht, Oppi. *Enameling on Metal.* New York: Greenberg Publishers, 1957.

Weiss, Harvey. *Clay, Wood, and Wire.* New York: William R. Scott, Inc., 1956.

————. *Paper, Ink and Roller.* New York: William R. Scott, Inc., 1958.

————. *Pencil, Pen and Brush.* New York: William R. Scott, Inc., 1961.

————. *Sticks, Spools and Feathers.* New York: William R. Scott, Inc., 1962.

Winebrenner, D. Kenneth. *Jewelry Making as an Art Expression.* Scranton, Pa.: International Textbook Co., 1953.

Winter, Ed. *Enameling for Beginners.* Worcester, Mass.: Creative Hands Bookshop, 1962.

Young, Joseph L. *Course in Making Mosaics.* New York: Reinhold Publishing Corp., 1957.

RECOMMENDED SUPPLEMENTAL PUBLICATIONS

A *Study of Basic Costs Per Pupil for an Effective Art Program in Grades One to Six,* Elizabeth Foster. Related Arts Service, 511 Fifth Avenue, New York 17, New York.

A *Teacher's Guide: Arts and Activities in the Classroom,* F. Louis Hoover. Jones Publishing Company, 8150 North Central Park Avenue, Skokie, Illinois.

Art Education: Dimension Supplement. Box 2127, University of Michigan, Ann Arbor, Michigan.

Art for Children's Growing. Association for Childhood Education, 1200 15th Street, N.W., Washington, D. C.

Art for the Family, Victor D'Amico and Committee. The Museum of Modern Art, New York, New York, 1954.

Art Materials and Formulas, Art Bulletin #3 (1957). Wisconsin Cooperative, Room 147, State Capitol, Madison 2, Wisconsin.

Art Recipes, Doris E. Foley. F. A. Owen Publisher, Dansville, New York, 1960.

Canadian Eskimo Art (Cat. No. R2-160). Quest for Handcrafts Ltd., Victoria, B. C.

Planning Facilities for Art Instruction. National Education Association, 1201 Sixteenth Street, N.W., Washington D. C., 1961.

Children and the Fine Arts, Illinois Education Press Bulletin C-4. Office of Superintendent of Public Instruction, Springfield, Illinois.

Creative Art in an Education Clinic. School of Art, School of Education, Syracuse University, Syracuse, New York.

Drawing and Painting as Expression, Art Bulletin #2, Curr. Bulletin #9 (1950). Wisconsin Co-op Educational Planning Program, Room 147 N, State Capitol, Madison 2, Wisconsin.

E Z Bulletin Boards, Anne Douglas Weseloh. Fearon Publishers, 828 Valencia Street, San Francisco 10, California.

Films on Art, Theodore Bowie. Audio Visual Center, Indiana University, Bloomington, Indiana, 1956.

Gallery Book for Children, Marie Zoe Greene. Department of Education, The Art Institute of Chicago, Chicago Illinois.

Ich Selbst, Myself, Moi-meme (Self portraits by children of several countries). Distributed by Artext Prints, Inc., Westport, Connecticut.

Basic Principles of Design. Pattern and Texture. Modern Art: Old and New. Modern Sculpture. What is Modern

Design? Museum of Modern Art, 11 West 53rd Street, New York 19, New York.

Teacher's Idea Book, L. R. Kohls. Art Education Department, Des Moines Art Center, Des Moines, Iowa.

Your Child and His Art, Viktor Lowenfeld. The Macmillan Company, New York, New York, 1957.

Your Child from 6 to 12, Children's Bureau Publication #324 (1949). Superintendent of Documents, U.S. Government Printing Office, Washington 25, D. C.

RECOMMENDED STATE AND CITY CURRICULUM GUIDES

Creative Art. Denver Public Schools, Denver, Colorado, 1949.

Art Education—Elementary Schools. Independent Community School District, Des Moines, Iowa, 1961.

Children Learn and Grow through Art Experiences, Bulletin C-4. Office of Superintendent of Public Instruction, Springfield, Illinois, 1958.

A Guide for Teaching Art: Grades Five and Six. Los Angeles City Schools, Curriculum Branch, Board of Education, Los Angeles, California, 1955.

Art Education for the Elementary Schools. State Department of Education, Columbus, Ohio, 1954.

Art Education in Oregon Elementary Schools. State Department of Education, Salem, Oregon, 1958.

Art—A Concept of Education. Pasadena, California, 1954. Distributor: Vroman's School Book Depository, Pasadena, California.

Growth Through Art. Milwaukee Public Schools, Division of Curriculum and Instruction, Milwaukee, Wisconsin, 1959.

Art for the Elementary Schools of Missouri, Pub. No. 1028. State Department of Education, Jefferson, Missouri, 1956.

The Child Creates, Bulletin #3. State Department of Education, Sante Fe, New Mexico, 1958.

Elementary Art Guide. State of Washington, Superintendent of Public Instruction, Olympia, Washington, 1961.

Art. Kindergarten, Grades One and Two, Publication No. EC212. Division of Instructional Services, Los Angeles City Schools, Los Angeles, California.

Art for Richmond's Children. Art Department, Richmond Public Schools, Richmond, Virginia.

RECOMMENDED PERIODICALS

Artist Junior, published bi-monthly by Artist Junior Publications, New Haven, Connecticut.

Arts and Activities, published monthly, except July and August, by Publisher's Development Corporation, 8150 North Central Park Avenue, Skokie, Illinois.

Ceramics Monthly, published monthly except July and August by Professional Publications, Inc., 4175 North High Street, Columbus 14, Ohio.

Craft Horizons, published bi-monthly by American Craftsmen's Council, 44 West 53rd Street, New York 19, New York.

Creative Crafts, published bi-monthly by Oxford Press, 6015 Santa Monica Boulevard, Los Angeles 38, California.

Design Quarterly, published by the Walker Art Center, Minneapolis, Minnesota.

Everyday Art, published quarterly by American Crayon Company, Sandusky, Ohio.

School Arts, published monthly, September through June, by The Davis Press, Worcester 8, Massachusetts.

RESOURCE PERIODICALS

Family Circle	*Look*
Holiday	*National Geographic*
House and Garden	*Popular Photography*
House Beautiful	*Sports Illustrated*
Life	*Woman's Day*

appendix D

RECOMMENDED FILMS, COLOR SLIDES, REPRODUCTIONS, AND RECORDINGS

RECOMMENDED FILMS FOR THE ELEMENTARY ART PROGRAM

The letters following each reference indicate films suitable for use in primary grades (P), in intermediate grades (I), in upper grades (U), and those appropriate for all grades (A). All films are 16 mm. with sound. The list which follows gives complete addresses of film sources referred to here by initials.

Adventuring in the Arts. Color—22 min. Distributed by Girl Scouts of America.

Animals. Color—11 min. IFB. Imaginary animals from papier-mâché, odds and ends. (U)

Around My Way. Color—11 min. CON. New York City as seen in children's drawings. (I)

Art in Motion. Color—17 min. EBF. To enrich child's design awareness. (U)

Art in Our World. Color—11 min. BAILEY. To expand the child's art horizons. (U)

Artist and Nature. Color—11 min. IFB. Shows how artists are inspired by nature's forms. (U)

Begone Dull Care. Color—9 min. IFB. A visual delight, color patterns set to contemporary jazz music. (A)

Behind the Scenes of a Museum. B/W—24 min. IFB. A short visit to the Natural History Museum of Chicago. (U)

Birds and Etching. Color—5 min. BAILEY. Simple etching and engraving processes. (U)

Buma: African Sculpture Speaks. Color—10 min. EBF. A colorful interpretation of selected African masks. (U)

Care of Art Materials. B/W—11 min. Young America Films, Inc. (A)

Children Are Creative. Color—16 min. BAILEY. For the elementary teacher, for parent meetings, and for in-service workshops.

Children Who Draw. B/W with Color—38 min. 1 Wanami Films. Japan. Japanese children in art activities.

Copper Enameling. Color—15 min. AHC (free).

Crayon Resist. Color—6 min. IFB. Varied processes of crayon resist. (U)

Design to Music. Color—5½ min. IFB. Children painting to music. (A)

Discovering Color. Discovering Texture. Color—15 min. FAC. Excellent films for both student and teacher enrichment. (U)

Eskimo Arts and Crafts. Color—22 min. IFB. (U)

Fiddle Dee Dee. Color—4 min. IFB. Norman MacLaren interprets sprightly violin music via color abstraction. (A)

Finger Painting of Wu Tsai-yen. Color—8 min. IFB. (U)

Indian Ceremonials. Color—18 min. SF. A dance by Indians of the Southwest. (A)

Insects and Painting. Color—5 min. BAILEY. Shows relationship between nature and painting in a child's work. (U)

Ink and Rice Paper. Color—15 min. Wood block demonstration. (U)

Lascaux, Cradle of Man's Art. Color—17 min. IFB. A documentary of prehistoric Cro-Magnon cave paintings. (U)

Light Reflections. Color—14 min. Technique of Jim Davis; unusual color abstractions using color acetates, motion, and light. (U)

Little Blue and Little Yellow. Color—10 min. CON. Color-facts illustrated in a whimsical way. (P)

Loon's Necklace. Color—15 min. EBF. An Indian legend told via ceremonial masks of the North Pacific Indians.

Make a Mobile. Color—11 min. IFB. Utilization of many materials for simple mobiles. (U)

Making a Mask. Color—6 min. IFB. Papier-mâché masks. (U)

Monotype Prints. Color—6 min. IFB. Simple one-impression printmaking. (U)

Mosaics. Color—19 min. AHC (free). (U)

Peter and the Potter. Color—21 min. IFB. A youngster's introduction to the fascination of pottery making. (U)

Picture in Your Mind. Color—16 min. IFB. To expand the child's visual awareness and sensitivity. (U)

Pin Mold. B/W—10 min. IFB Study of microscopic world which influences contemporary artists. (U)

Report in Primary Colors. Color—20 min. FPS. For elementary teachers, parents, and in-service meetings and workshops.

The Sumi Artist. Color—15 min. LOBETT. Chiura Obata demonstrates traditional Japanese painting technique. (U)

Torn Paper. Color—6 min. IFM. Simple torn-paper techniques. (U)

Totems. Color—11 min. IFB. Totem carvings by Indians of British Columbia. (U)

A Trip to the Moon. Color—14 min. BRAN. Children of various countries paint their interpretation of a trip to the moon. (A)

Weeds and Mosaics. Color—5 min. BAILEY. Simple mosaic techniques with "found" materials. (U)

What Shall We Paint? Color—10 min. FAC. (A)

ADDRESSES OF FILM COMPANIES

AHC	American Handicrafts Co., 83 West Van Buren Street, Chicago 5, Illinois.
AF	Associated Films, 247 Madison Avenue, New York 7, New York.
BAILEY	Bailey Films, 6509 De Longpre Avenue, Hollywood 28, California.
BRAN	Brandon Films, Inc., 200 W. 57th Street, New York 19, New York.
CON	Contemporary Films, Inc., 267 W. 25th Street, New York 1, New York.
EBF	Encyclopedia Brittanica Films, Wilmette, Illinois.
FAC	Film Associates of California, 11014 Santa Monica Blvd., Los Angeles 25, California.
FPS	Film Production Service, Virginia Dept. of Education, Richmond 16, Virginia.
IFB	International Film Bureau, Inc., 332 South Michigan Avenue, Chicago 4, Illinois.
LOBETT	Lobett Productions, 2002 Taraval Street, San Francisco 16, California.
SF	Sante Fe Film Bureau, 80 Jackson Blvd., Chicago 4, Illinois.
Also recommended:	French Cultural Services, 972 Fifth Avenue, New York 21, New York.

COLOR SLIDE SOURCES

American Library Color Slide Co. Inc., 222 West 23rd Street, New York 11, New York.

Art Council Aids, Box 641, Beverly Hills, California. *Emotion Takes Form. Children Paint Their World.*

Dr. Konrad Prothman, 2787 Milburn Avenue, Baldwin, L. I., New York. *Italian Children's Painting. Growth Through Art. Child Art—U.S.A. Art is Everywhere. Three-Dimensional Expression.*

Museum of Modern Art Library, 11 West 53rd Street, New York 19, New York.

Philadelphia Museum of Art, Division of Education, Parkway at 26th, Philadelphia 30, Pennsylvania.

School of the Art Institute of Chicago, Chicago, Illinois.

DEALERS IN COLOR REPRODUCTIONS AND PRINTS
(Catalogs or brochures available)

Artext Prints, Inc., Westport, Connecticut.

Associated American Artists, Inc., 711 Fifth Avenue, New York 22, New York.

Catalda Fine Arts, Inc., 225 Fifth Avenue, New York 10, New York.

FAR Gallery, 702 Madison Avenue, New York 21, New York.

Esther Gentle, 40 East 49th Street, New York, New York.

Penn Prints, Harlem Book Company, Inc., 221 Park Avenue South, New York 3, New York.

Metropolitan Museum of Art, Art and Book Shop, Fifth Avenue and 82nd Street, New York 28, New York.

New York Graphic Society, 10 West 33rd Street, New York 1, New York.

Oestreicher's, 1208 Sixth Avenue, New York, New York.

Dr. Konrad Prothmann, 7 Soper Avenue, Baldwin, Long Island, New York.

Raymond and Raymond, Inc., 40 East 52nd Street, New York 22, New York.

Urban Prints, 234 East 58th Street, New York, New York.

E. Weyhe, 794 Lexington Avenue, New York 21, New York.

RECOMMENDED MUSICAL RECORDINGS

Musical Recordings, both rhythmic and descriptive, suggested for correlated art activities.

An American in Paris (Gershwin)
Appalachian Spring (Copland)
Bolero (Ravel)
Brass and Percussion
Carnival of the Animals (Saint-Saëns)
Flight of the Bumblebee (Rimski-Korsakov)
Gaite Parisienne (Offenbach)
March of the Toys (Herbert)
Marches in Hi-Fi
Mexican Hat Dance
Nutcracker Suite (Tchaikovsky)
Overtures on Parade
Peter and the Wolf (Prokofiev)
Petroushka (Stravinsky)
Pop goes the Weasel
Ritual Fire Dance (Falla)
Rodeo (Copland)
Sabre Dance (Khachaturian)
Scheherazade (Rimski-Korsakov)
Swan Lake (Tchaikovsky)
Syncopated Clock (Anderson)
The Sorceror's Apprentice (Dukas)

Dried autumn plants of many varieties can be found to use in still-life compositions.

MATERIALS

NEW USES FOR "FOUND" MATERIALS

When teachers consider supplies for art activities, they generally think first in terms of materials commercially and specifically produced for the art class. A wealth of objects is found all around us, things not commonly thought of as art supplies but that somehow can be utilized in the art program. Most of the items listed below can be found in basements, attics, garages, school shops, machine shops, radio shops, or even the city junk yard. Children should be encouraged to bring in scrap materials and "found" objects. Shoe boxes, cigar boxes, and half-gallon and gallon milk or ice cream containers will serve for storage of these materials. "Found" materials enrich the art program and expand its horizons, especially when the school is operating on a limited budget, but the discriminating teacher must use taste and caution to make sure that the "found" objects do not wind up in "lost" expressions.

Material or Object	Possible Use in Art Program	Material or Object	Possible Use in Art Program
Asbestos, powdered	Mixed with wheat paste as a modeling substance	Boxes, assorted cardboard and paper	Construction work; storage files; storage for constructions
Bags, paper	Paper bag masks; puppet heads	Boxes, cheese, wooden	Storage; decorated for gift projects
Balloons	Mobiles; foundations for papier-mâché forms or paper sculpture	Boxes, cigar	Storage; box construction
		Boxes, round oatmeal	Box construction; bases for totem poles
Balls, rubber, ping-pong, basketball	Mobiles; constructions	Boxes, suit	Light construction work; mobiles; cardboard prints
Bamboo curtain remnants	Collage; construction; ink drawing tools	Buckles	Scrap metal construction
Bark from trees	Collage	Buckram	Collage
Beads	Constructions; collage	Bulbs, light	Puppet heads; metal constructions
Beans, dried	Collage		
Blades, razor (single-edge)	Constructions; crayon engraving; stick and reed stabiles	Bulbs, photoflash	Metal construction; heads for figures, animals
Blades, saw (broken)	Making textures in clay or plaster	Buttons	Scrap constructions; collage
		Buttons, metal	Metal constructions; animals
Blinds, matchstick	Collage; constructions; stabiles	Candles	Crayon encaustic; resist projects
Blocks, wooden	Constructions; bases; imprinting	Cans, tin	Paint; water containers; metal construction
Blotters	Collage; printmaking to blot paper	Canvas	Collage; wedging board surface
Board, peg	Collage; constructions	Caps, bottle	Construction; collage; imprinting pieces
Bolts and nuts	Constructions in metal; imprinting pieces for clay	Cardboard from shirts (laundry)	Paper sculpture; cardboard printing; multi-crayon engraving
Bones	Imprinting pieces; still-life material	Cardboard, corrugated	Constructions; collages
Book jackets	Paper mosaic tesserae; collage	Carpet samples	Collage; texture printing
		Cartons, egg	Collages; masks; box construction
Bottles, small colored	Mosaics; plaster reliefs		

Material or Object	Possible Use in Art Program	Material or Object	Possible Use in Art Program
Cartons, ice cream—round, all sizes to 10 gal.	Scrap material containers; plaster of Paris molds	Cups, paper	Paper construction
Catalogs	Pasting surfaces; colored backgrounds for print surfaces; tesserae sources	Dental tools (discarded)	Engraving on plaster; crayon engraving
		Depressors, tongue	Collage; construction
Cellophane (colored)	Collages; transparent pictorial designs	Dominoes	Imprinting pieces
		Drapery samples or remnants	Collage; stuffed animals; papier-mâché decoration
Celotex	Working surface for reed constructions	Egg separators	Constructions; collage
Chains	Constructions; making impressions in clay	Embroidery hoops	For simple silk screen prints
		Emery cloth	Craft projects; collage
Checkers	Constructions; making impressions in clay	Erasers	Printmaking
		Feathers	Collage; imprinting; printmaking
Clips, paper	Construction	Felt	Collage
Clock works	Metal constructions; making impressions in clay	Filler, rug	Stitchery; collage
		Filters, metal	Metal construction
Cloth, cheese, terry cloth remnants	Collage; patina application; burnishing	Fish net	Collage; stitchery; still-life arrangements
Coins	Imprinting pieces	Flowers, dried	Source material for drawing, painting
Combs	Making impressions in clay; crayon engraving		
Cones, fir	Imprinting pieces; collage	Foam rubber	Collage; printmaking
Cones, paper	Paper sculpture	Foil, aluminum or tin	Metal construction; repoussé reliefs
Confetti	Collage	Fur	Collage
Containers, waxed cardboard milk	Molds for plaster carving blocks	Gauze, theatrical	Stitchery; collage
Cord	Collage; printmaking; stitchery; plaster masks; mobiles	Grog	Ceramic projects, aggregate for plaster of Paris molds
		Grounds, coffee	Collage
Corks, all sizes	Constructions; mobiles	Hangers, wire coat	Metal construction, armature
Corn, dried	Collage	Inner tubing	Collage; printmaking
Cotton warp	Stitchery; collage	Jewelry	Metal construction

Material or Object	Possible Use in Art Program	Material or Object	Possible Use in Art Program
Keys	Collage; clay reliefs; metal construction	Paper, pulp trays	Collage; masks; box construction
Lath, wire	Metal stabiles; mobiles	Paper, tar, building	Collage; construction
Leather scraps	Collage	Paper towels	Blotting tempera batiks; papier-mâché; collage
Leaves, real and plastic	Stencil; printmaking		
Lids, jar	Metal construction; mobiles	Paper, waxed	Multiple purposes
Linoleum	Collage; construction; printmaking	Paper, wrapping, shelf	Tempera painting; printing; collage
Machine parts	Metal constructions; making impressions in clay	Pebbles and stones	Mosaic; collage
		Pins	Multiple purposes
Magazine advertisements	Collage; printing surfaces; paper mosaics	Pins, hair and clothes	Constructions; imprinting
		Pins, hat	Tools for crayon engraving
Marbles	Metal constructions; metal enameling	Pipe cleaners	Armatures for small papier-mâché figures; collage
Masonite remnants	Collage; constructions; inking squares	Plastic scraps	Collage; metal constructions
		Plywood	Collage; constructions; bases
Mats, rubber floor	Collage; printmaking	Poles, fishing	Inking pens from thin segments
Mica	Collage		
Mirrors (discarded)	Self-portrait drawing	Polish, shoe and furniture	Stains and patinas on clay, plaster, and papier-mâché sculpture
Nails (assorted)	Imprinting pieces, engraving tools; constructions		
Neckties	Collage; puppets; stuffed animals	Radio parts	Metal stabiles; mobiles; to make impressions in clay
Netting, chicken	Collage; stitchery	Raffia	Hair for masks or puppets
Newspapers	Multiple purposes	Reed	Collage; construction; clay imprinting
Nut picks (discarded)	Engraving tools		
Oilcloth	Clay projects; fingerpainting surface	Ribbons	Collage; puppets
		Rings, jar	Construction; mobiles
Paper, newspaper	Several layers of newspapers moistened with wheat paste can be shaped for masks	Rope	Collage; construction
		Rubber, innertube	Collage; printmaking
		Rug remnants	Collage; texture printing
		Salt	Collage; modeling mixture

MATERIAL OR OBJECT	POSSIBLE USE IN ART PROGRAM	MATERIAL OR OBJECT	POSSIBLE USE IN ART PROGRAM
Sandpaper	Collage; surface for crayoning constructions	Tile, vinyl	Collage; constructions
Screws	Metal constructions; imprinting	Tinker toys	Constructions, imprinting pieces
Sea shells	Imprinting	Tins, pie, cookie	Paint mixing palettes; metal construction
Seeds	Collage	Toothbrushes	Cleaning plaster reliefs, castings
Shades, window	Collage; painting or printing surface	Toothpicks	Constructions; collage; ink sketching
Sheeting, cork	Collage; construction; printmaking	Trays (TV dinner)	Paint mixing palettes
Sheeting, metal (copper, tin)	Repoussé reliefs, metal construction	Tubes, mailing	Construction armatures; box sculpture
Shingles, tar	Collage; construction	Tubing, rubber	Scrap construction; printmaking
Shot	Collage	Twigs	Armatures for papier-mâché; scrap construction
Silk	Collage; stitchery and appliqué	Vermiculite (aggregate)	Collage
Sponge, metal, plastics	Imprinting pieces	Wallpaper	Paint or print on reverse side; collage
Sponge, rubber	Collage; texture painting and printing	Wax, floor	Protect surfaces of fired clay, papier-mâché, wood sculpture
Spools, thread	Constructions; printing tool		
Springs	Metal constructions		
Steel wool	Cleaning and burnishing metals; metal constructions	Weeds	Still life
		Wire, copper, insulated, chicken, stove pipe	Metal constructions
Sticks, pick-up, applicator, paste	Collage; construction	Wood, all kinds	Constructions; collage; bases; wood block prints
Straws, cellophane, waxed	Constructions; mobiles	Wood, drift	Displays; sculpture
Thread	Stitchery; collage; construction	X-ray plates, used	Collage; construction; printmaking
Thumbtacks and tacks	Multiple uses	Yarn	Collage; construction; stitchery
Tile, acoustic	Making surface for reed forms; collage; constructions		

SOME SPECIAL MATERIALS, SUGGESTED SOURCES, AND USES

MATERIAL	USE	SOURCE
Applicator sticks	For constructions; stabile; mobiles	Drug store, hospital supply firm
Aggregate (Perlite, Zonolite, vermiculite, Terra-lite)	Mix with plaster of Paris for textural effects and ease in carving; also for collage	Lumber dealer
Beaverboard (Upson board) 1/4 or 1/8 inch	To protect table tops or for drawing boards; overlap edges with masking tape for longer wear; coat with latex paint, if desired	Lumber dealer
Burlap (in assorted colors)	For stitchery; appliqué; collage; or display	Department and mail order stores
Celotex, 1/2 inch	As surface for working reed and stick stabiles	Lumber dealer
Cement (Testor Formula AA, fast-drying airplane glue)	For reed, stick, toothpick constructions	Local stores, art and craft shops
Craypas	Combination crayon and pastel medium for picture making at all levels	Art store
Dextrin	Adhesive in powder form; add 5 or 10 percent to moist clay to achieve hardening without firing	Drug store
Easycurve board	Constructions where a heavy yet pliable board is needed	Lumber dealer
Featherock	A lightweight gray, porous pumice or lava stone adaptable for upper elementary carving projects	Featherock Inc. 6331 Hollywood Blvd. Los Angeles 28, Calif.
Firebrick	A lightweight, porous refractory brick for carving projects	Lumber yard
Formaldehyde	A few drops in liquid media (tempera, fingerpaint, or monoprint medium) will prevent souring. Phenol can be substituted for similar results	Drug store

MATERIAL	USE	SOURCE
Gauze with plaster additive	For plaster of Paris constructions, and masks	Hospital supply firm
Gesso	Plaster of Paris solution conditioned with glue, for coating of papier-mâché creations	Art store
Glue (liquid white) clear-drying	As a protective coating or seal on plaster sculpture before staining	Lumber, paint, or art store
Glycerin	Mix with honey and powdered tempera for a monoprint medium	Drug store
Markers, felt nib	Refillable markers in assorted colors for drawing and painting	Art supply store
Muraltex board (24- by 36-inch)	A strong, textured paper for tempera painting, Sketcho compositions, and small mural projects	Consolidated Supply Co. Columbus, Ohio
Paraffin	For coating cardboard box molds prior to plaster casting	Local store
Paris craft	Plaster-impregnated gauze in varied widths for 3-D constructions over armatures or papier-mâché forms	Art supply store
Plaster of Paris (molding plaster)	For making carving molds, reliefs, spoon jewelry, applied sculpture	Lumber dealer
Plastic covers (elasticized, 6 inches in diameter, clear)	For covers on tempera cups	Boland Mfg. Co. Winona, Minnesota
Polymer medium	A painting vehicle used especially for glazing; can be diluted with water	Art supply store
Rub 'n' Buff	Metallic finishes for sculpture, reliefs, jewelry, ceramics. Turpentine is solvent.	Art supply store
Sculpmetal	For patina on papier-mâché or sculptured pieces. Apply in diluted form; when dry coat with India ink and burnish with steel wool	Art supply firm

MATERIAL	USE	SOURCE
Shreddimix	For papier-mâché constructions and low relief composition	Art supply store
Sloyd knife	A strong, short-bladed, blunt knife, excellent for carving projects	Brodhead-Garrett Co. Cleveland, Ohio
Tissue paper (assorted colors—swatch available)	For tissue collage; reed and stick constructions; printmaking surfaces	Austen Display Co. 133 West 19th Street New York 11, New York
Tongue depressors	For paint mixers; construction projects; clay modeling	Drug store, hospital supply firm
Transfer paper (white dressmaker's)	For transfer of preliminary drawings or sketches to dark surfaces	Orco Products Inc. 275 Leo Street Dayton 4, Ohio
Wood stain	For staining ceramic pieces, plaster of Paris sculpture, and gesso-coated papier-mâché works	Paint store

appendix

F

FACILITIES FOR
ELEMENTARY ART

The qualitative program in elementary school art depends in great part on adequate, functional facilities for instruction. There will necessarily be adaptations of art facilities for the self-contained classroom, where art is taught one or two periods a week, as contrasted with the multipurpose art room, where many art classes are taught each day. But if certain minimum art facility requirements are met in the plans of the self-contained classrooms yet to be built, the climate for growth in art in the elementary schools of the future should be a more favorable one. Basically, the changes that need to be made are in the areas of room size, adequate storage, display space, and clean-up facilities.

LOCATION OF THE ART ROOM

The multipurpose art room should preferably be on the first or ground floor, adjacent to the stage of the auditorium, and near a service entrance. An outdoor court, easily accessible from the art room via sliding doors, can provide excellent auxiliary space for sketching, mural making, ceramics, construction, and sculpture in favorable weather.

SPACE ALLOTMENT

The multipurpose art room should provide at least 35 to 40 square feet per pupil as a minimum, excluding storage space. In essence, enough space should be provided to allow students to work on individual projects with some flexibility of movement, to permit rearrangement of furniture for group projects, and to ensure an efficient flow of traffic to storage and clean-up areas.

The self-contained classroom should provide additional space at the rear of the room and along the window wall for storage, clean-up facilities, and counter surface working areas. There should also be enough room at the back of the classroom for one or more large project tables.

FUNCTIONAL FURNITURE

Whether in the self-contained classroom or the special art room, nonglare, waterproof, and scratch-resistant horizontal desk or table surfaces are recommended. Tables or desks should be adjustable in height and easily movable to provide for group or project activities. In the multipurpose art room, backless, adjustable-height stools which can slide under the tables to provide more traffic room are often desirable. In the lower elementary grades free-standing easels can effectively augment the limited desk space.

ADEQUATE STORAGE

Storage facilities are a critical factor in expediting a qualitative program in art. There should be adequate storage for art supplies, tools, visual aids, projects in process, and completed projects used in display. These facilities can range from simple to elaborate in purpose and structure.

Art supply storage should be provided for assorted art papers (drawers with inside measurements slightly larger than the size of the paper); tempera, watercolors, chalk, inks, paste, brushes (adjustable shelves are recommended for these supplies); yarn, wood, plastics, "found objects" (bin-type storage or tote-tray cabinet); clay (movable, rustproof, air-tight bins or galvanized garbage cans).

A cabinet or movable cart is suggested for tool storage. A simple pegboard panel and hardware hanging facilities will suffice in most situations. Painting an identifying shape or outline of the tool on the panel will help expedite storage.

Since much of the children's artwork involves painting, there should be adequate horizontal storage for projects in process. This is especially true in the multipurpose art room, where one class follows another and thus the working surfaces must be cleared quickly. There are a number of horizontal storage facilities on the market, but a simple, flat storage unit can be constructed of a framework of ¾-inch plywood and pull-out shelves of masonite, plywood, or Upson board. A clothesline and spring-type clothespins may be utilized as a drying facility for wet vegetable, cardboard, or linoleum prints.

A definite problem in the self-contained classroom is the storage of *three-dimensional* projects in process, such as clay figures or pots, paper, papier-mâché or box sculpture, stabiles, and mobiles. Counter space above storage cabinets, the floor area around the room, and closet shelves are possibilities. Tote-tray facilities could provide another possible solution. Mobiles in process or on display should, if possible, be hung from special ceiling hooks, but wire or clothesline strung from the tops of doors or windows may serve the purpose. Hanging mobiles from lighting fixtures should be discouraged, since it may prove hazardous.

CLEAN-UP FACILITIES

In order to reduce traffic problems, the sink area should be easily accessible from all parts of the room. It should not be located in a corner or closet. The sink (a peninsula or island type is recommended) should be stainproof and easily cleaned, with multiple mixing faucets and heavy duty drains and sink traps to prevent clogging of the plumbing. It should be large enough to allow several youngsters to use it at the same time. It should be low enough so that the children can reach the faucets with ease, or it should be provided with a step-up platform.

DISPLAY FACILITIES

A maximum amount of space should be available for display purposes and instructional bulletin boards. This holds true for both the self-contained classroom and the multipurpose art room. Display backgrounds should be neutral in color. Subtle whites, grays, or pastels, and occasionally black, are recommended. Surfaces should be nonglare, with easy pinning qualities, such as cork or Celotex. Random-punch butt-end acoustic tile can be glued directly to walls or to masonite panels with tile adhesive to form a simple, yet effective, display facility. Cork-surfaced doors on cupboards and cabinets will augment the display potential. It is advisable to keep one classroom wall entirely free for display or mural possibilities. Recessed cabinets, both in classroom and in hallway, can provide safe, three-dimensional display space.

OTHER SPECIFICATIONS

Other factors important in the planning of the elementary art room are:

Floors should be of nonskid material, hard but resilient and easily cleaned. Neutral-colored asphalt or plastic tile is often recommended.

Ceilings should be acoustically treated and provide maximum light reflection.

Lighting, both natural and artificial, should be provided so that there is sufficient light intensity for the requirements of the students with a minimum of glare.

Room-darkening shades or *blinds* should be installed to expedite the visual aids program.

White "blackboards" can aid effectively in presenting art lessons in a positive "black and white" interpretation. Easily cleaned, these boards can also be used as screens for slide or film projection.

Electrical outlets should be provided at intervals around the room. These should be wired for 110 volts. If a clay or enamel kiln is to be used, the voltage for those facilities should be higher. Electrical outlets should not be installed adjacent to sinks.

SPECIAL EQUIPMENT

Whether in the self-contained classroom or in the multipurpose art room, special equipment and furniture is often needed to implement a rich and varied program. The following items are often recommended:

Clay bin or cart
Vibrating jig saw
Workbench with vise
Electric heating plate
Utility cart
Paper cutter
Free-standing easels
Color slide projector and screen
Ceramic kiln
Metal enameling kiln

G

GLOSSARY
OF TERMS

Abstract art—an interpretation that expresses the essence of a figure, object, or place in lines, geometric forms, or planes with little regard for its natural appearance.

Acetone—a solvent for plastics.

Aesthetic—appreciative of, or responsive to, the beautiful in art or nature.

Alcohol—a solvent for shellac (methanol or shellacol).

Armature—framework used to support modeling substances such as clay, papier-mâché, or plaster (usually made of wood, metal, or wire mesh).

Asymmetric—a balance in art composition based on an informal or occult relationship.

Balsa—a strong, light wood for carving, construction, model building, or for collages (available in sheets, strips, or blocks).

Bas-relief—low relief sculpture (the opposite of incised relief).

Bat—a flat, level plaster slab used to absorb moisture from wet clay. (A bat can be easily cast by pouring prepared plaster of Paris into a vaseline-coated rubberized dishpan.)

Batik—a method of creating colored designs on fabric by coating with wax those areas not to be dyed (term also used to describe resist techniques).

Biomorphic—related to life or living organisms.

Bisque—unglazed pottery after first firing.

Bit—a tool used with a brace for drilling or boring.

Brayer—rubber roller used in inking printing blocks (gelatin brayers are also available).

Buffer—a line, shape, value, or color that redirects the eye movement in a picture composition.

Burnish—to make smooth or shiny by a rubbing or polishing action.

Burr—a rough ridge in metal, clay, or other substances created by a gouging tool passing through the surface area.

Chipboard—heavy cardboard or poster board, usually gray, for use in painting, collage, construction, and cardboard prints.

Chroma—another designation for color or hue.

Collage—composition made by assembling, pasting, and gluing materials to a surface (can be combined with drawing, painting, and glazing).

Colors: *Primary*—red, yellow, blue; three basic hues which cannot be produced by a mixture of pigments.

Secondary—orange, green, purple; colors achieved by mixing primaries.

Tertiary—colors derived by mixing secondaries; sometimes called intermediate hues.

Analogous—colors, closely related, neighbors on the color wheel—yellow, orange, red, for example.

Complementary—colors opposite each other on the color wheel—sharply contrasting hues.

Triad—colors equidistant from each other on the color wheel.

Warm—colors usually associated with fire, sun, and earth—red, brown, orange.

Cool—colors usually associated with water, sky, spring, and foliage—green, blue, turquoise.

Contour—a line drawing delineating the external characteristics or boundaries of a shape or form.

Coping saw—a small hand saw used to cut circular and irregular shapes in plywood, Upson board, masonite, and heavy cardboards.

Design—an ordered, aesthetic arrangement of one or more of the components of art—line, value, shape, form, color, or texture.

Distortion—deliberate or intuitive alteration by the artist of a natural shape, form, or surface.

Dowel—a thin pole of wood available in graded diameters.

Empathy—the projection of one's personality into the object of contemplation, a feeling into.

Emphasis—a principle in design or composition which connotes importance or significance. It often implies both dominance and subordination.

Engobe—liquid clay or slip applied as color for surface decoration in ceramics; should be applied while clay is damp.

Engraving—the process of incising or scratching into metal or other prepared surfaces with a sharp tool.

Expression—in art, a subjective interpretation of sensations, emotions, or ideas, rather than of actual appearances.

Fixative—a commercial preparation in liquid or spray form used to protect easily-smudged surfaces.

Flux—a material applied to a point to be soldered to prevent oxides from forming when the metal is heated.

Focal point—a point or spot of interest in a composition where the observer's eye comes to rest.

Foreshortening—the apparent visual compression or distortion of forms in a composition to indicate depth in space.

Form—usually a sculptural or three-dimensional shape defined by its characteristic contour.

Fresco—a painting on freshly applied plaster (true fresco).

Frottage—a design created by rubbing a grease or wax crayon on thin paper placed over objects with raised surface qualities, such as reliefs, mosaics, collages, or natural forms like feathers, grained wood, leaves, bark, or seaweed.

Gelatin—transparent theatrical color modulator available in multiple colors.

Genre—compositions which emphasize themes of domestic and everyday events.

Glaze—a transparent or opaque surface finish applied to ceramic or metalware.

Greenware—unfired ceramic ware.

Grog—fired clay ground to a powder; provides porosity and texture in clay pieces to be fired.

Hatching—a system for building up tones or shadows by using a series of lines at various angles (crosshatching).

Horizon line—an imaginary line, usually at the eye level of the observer, where the sky seems to meet the earth.

Hue—color.

Impasto—a particularly thick or heavy application of paint.

Intaglio—an engraved design, the opposite of relief.

Intensity—in reference to color, the brightness or dullness of the hue.

Kiln—an oven or furnace for drying, firing, or glazing ceramic ware (also metal enamelling kiln).

Line—a mark made by a moving point.

Lithography—a process of printing from a stone or prepared metal plate involving the use of a grease crayon and ink.

Local color—the positive or natural color of an object, for example, leaf-green, lemon-yellow, sky-blue.

Lost wax process—a method of casting in metal those objects which are first made in clay or wax.

Masonite—a pressed board made from steam-exploded wood fibers; can be used for drawing boards, clay boards, inking surfaces, and construction projects.

Mass—a large form or a substantial area of color or value.

Mat board—heavy poster board used for mounting pictures, specimens, and other displays.

Matte (or mat)—a term describing a dull, flat, nonglossy surface or sheen.

Medium—any material used for art expression, such as clay, paint, wood, or metal.

Mobile—a kind of sculpture in which the parts move; usually of metal.

Monochromatic—referring to a one-color interpretation.

Monoprint—a type of surface printing in which the design is created on a hard surface such as glass with oil, ink, or fingerpaint. The composition is then transferred to the paper by contact.

Mosaic—a design or composition formed by the planned juxtaposition of clay or glass tesserae cemented in grout or mortar.

Motif—center or dominant theme or feature.

Mural—a wall painting, usually performing an architectonic function.

Nonobjective art—expressions of pure form design which bear no resemblance to natural objects.

Papier-mâché—a substance made of paper pulp conditioned with sizing or paste.

Pastel—another name for colored chalk or description for the tint of a color.

Plaster of Paris—a white powder (calcium sulfate) which when mixed with water forms a quick-setting casting or construction material.

Positive-Negative—positive areas in a composition are definite forms and shapes; negative areas are the unoccupied or empty spaces.

Radiation—divergent lines, forms, or colors emanating from a central point of interest.

Raffia—a palm fiber available in a wide range of colors.

Repoussé—metal work in which the design is hammered into a relief form from the reverse side.

Rhythm—an ordered movement made by the repetition of pictorial elements.

Rubber cement—a clean, quick-drying, latex type of cement or glue.

Scoring—to mark with grooves using an edged tool—as in paper sculpture or clay welding.

Scumble—a painting term referring to the softening of a color by the application of another opaque color over it.

Shape—area, form, or mass with a specific character and often defined by outline or contrast.

Solvent—a liquid which dissolves or reduces the viscosity of other liquids. (Turpentine is a solvent for oil paint.)

Space: three-dimensional—in art, a structure or form possessing thickness, or depth, as well as length and breadth.

Stabile—a design in space made of wire, string, or other affinitive materials, mounted on a base and having no moving parts (space modulator).

Symbol—in art, the representation of an object, idea, or quality through an intermediate figure, sign, or geometric character.

Tactile—referring to the sense of touch.

Tempera—an opaque, water-soluble paint in which the pigment is mixed with an albuminous substance.

Terra cotta—an earth-colored clay, generally unglazed.

Tessera—a small, geometric segment of glass, marble, stone, or similar material used in mosaic work.

Texture—the actual and/or visual feel of a surface; the representation of the tactile character of a given material.

Tint—a graduation of a color achieved by mixing it with white pigment or diluting it with a solvent.

Translucent—semi-opaque, partly transparent.

Value—an attribute of color, its lightness or darkness; for example, the values of red would range from pink to maroon.

Vanishing point—in perspective drawings, a point or points to which all lines recede.

Vermiculite—a form of mica or insulation material, generally used as an aggregate in plaster of Paris carving blocks (Zonolite, Perlite).

Vitrification—the process of becoming glass-like, as in a glaze, or nonporous, as in ceramics.

Volume—in art, usually a form or mass with three-dimensional or solid implications.

Wedging—a method of preparing clay by kneading it to expel air pockets and make it constantly plastic.

Welding—in clay modeling, the process of adhering two pieces of clay with slip and/or scoring procedures.

X-ray picture—in child art, the unique interpretation of places which are normally hidden from view, for example, a coal mine, gophers underground, a tunnel under the river.

Grade 1

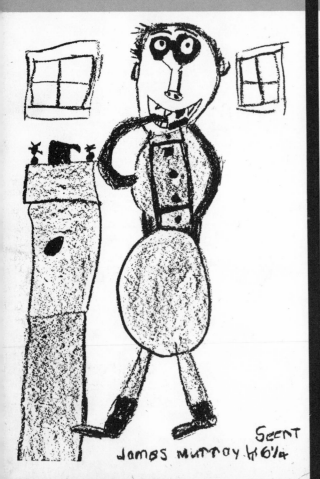

James, age six.

Grade 2

Drew, age eight.

Grade 3

Jeff, age nine.